HEAVEN AWAITS

Inspirational Daily Devotions

Bonnie Weber

ISBN 979-8-89309-547-0 (Paperback)
ISBN 979-8-89309-548-7 (Digital)

Copyright © 2024 Bonnie Weber
All rights reserved
First Edition

The New Chain-Reference Bible Fourth Improved Edition
Containing Thompson's Original and the
Complete System of Bible Study

Compiled and Edited by Frank Charles Thompson, DD, PhD

B. B. Kirkbridge, Bible Co., Inc. Indianapolis, Indiana, USA

© 1964

Fifty-Second Reprint

King James Version

All rights reserved. No part of this publication may be reproduced, distributed, or transmitted in any form or by any means, including photocopying, recording, or other electronic or mechanical methods without the prior written permission of the publisher. For permission requests, solicit the publisher via the address below.

Covenant Books
11661 Hwy 707
Murrells Inlet, SC 29576
www.covenantbooks.com

This book is dedicated to my parents, James and Norma Sahr, who raised me with the *love* of Jesus.

Special recognition goes to my husband, Scott, and our two children for their support, encouragement, and inspiration in writing this book.

For we walk by *faith*, not by sight.

—2 Corinthians 5:7

Heaven Awaits for you...

Bonnie

Heaven Awaits
for you...
Bonnie

Acknowledgements for contributing Bible verses (i.e., confirmation verses) to this book include: S. Weber, G. Weber, K. Weber, B. Weber, P. Weber, R. Hilger, G. Hilger, J. Hilger, A. Hilger, J. Sahr, N. Sahr, H. Weber, I. Weber, M. Sahr, S. Sahr, S. Kaufman, and P. McKeon.

Friends: N. Dixon, M. A. Ernest, D. Hill, E. Kast, B. Marker, K. Rollwagen, N. Salvner, E. Shaver, and J. Weiss.

Inspiration: S. Browning, R. Barritt, C. Davis, D. Duby, J. McIntosh, and D. Hauser.

JANUARY 1

> And Joshua said unto them, "Fear not, nor be dismayed, be strong and of good courage: for thus shall the Lord do to all your enemies against whom ye fight." (Joshua 10:25)

Calm your fears so you are not afraid. Do not let your fears control you. Be strong in God's Word. Read the Bible to calm your fears.

Be courageous and have a positive outlook on life. Face the day with Him by your side.

Look for new opportunities to face your fears by taking a walk, smiling at a stranger, or making new friendships with coworkers.

Reach for the opportunity God has given you. The experience may be just the spark that calms your fears.

*****

Dear Lord,

Calm my fears so I am not afraid to venture into this world alone. Keep me strong in your Word to face the challenges upon me. Amen.

JANUARY 2

> But he said, "Yea rather, blessed are they that hear the word of God and keep it." (Luke 11:28)

Feeling blessed is a unique experience. Expressing your gratitude to others opens many doors to share His Word.

Talk to friends and share your similarities. Meet monthly or more often for lunch or after work. Create a bond and then invite new friends to outings to form a larger circle of new friends.

Create a list of your blessings and compare the list, year by year, to see how it has changed. By next year at this time, you will be blessed plentiful.

*****

Dear Jesus,

Thank you for the many blessings you have bestowed upon me. You alone are the one who provides for me. Help me to appreciate the blessings I receive from you and always remember to thank you daily. Amen.

JANUARY 3

> Sing, O heavens; and be joyful, O earth;
> and break forth into singing, O mountains: for
> the Lord hath comforted his people and will have
> mercy upon his afflicted. (Isaiah 49:13)

Feel the assurance that you are right where you should be in your life. God is there to comfort you and guide you on the path to righteousness.

Not every day is a cheerful day; there could be down days when you need to be picked up.

Try searching the scripture for verses on comfort and thanking God for being with you on your good days and your bad days.

You may need to go to a separate room and have a conversation with God, out loud, without being interrupted. Just talking about your troubles, and asking for His comfort, may make you feel better.

*****

Dear Lord,

Continue to comfort me when trials and tribulations come into my life. Be with me to always focus on your word. Amen.

JANUARY 4

> Delight thyself also in the Lord; and he shall
> give thee the desires of thine heart. (Psalm 37:4)

As you live your life in the Lord, thank Him daily for giving you your life, your family, your friends, and your health.

Sometimes we take life for granted, and when a family member or close friend is taken from us, we realize too late how important they were to us. Make it a point to keep in touch with those who are important in your life.

Celebrate yourself and treat yourself to a special event or meal.

You are truly a delight in God's eyes; bask in your accomplishments and feel good about yourself.

*****

Dear God,

You alone see the delight in the work done by my accomplishments; be with me and protect me in all future endeavors so that they are pleasing to you. Amen.

JANUARY 5

> Be still and know that I am God: I will be exalted among the heathen, I will be exalted in the earth. (Psalm 46:10)

Have you ever been alone with God in prayer and wondered if your prayer will be answered? God does answer your prayers; it may not be the answer you wanted. God may have a different direction for answering your prayer.

When in prayer with God, put away cell phones and other distractions. Focus on your need and then take the time to listen. God encourages patience when we go to Him in prayer.

God will calm your anxieties and give you comfort. He asks us to "be still." Knowing God watches over us brings us such great comfort that He will not put us in any harm or danger.

*****

Dear God,

Thank you for protecting us from harm and danger. Be with us so we may exalt in your ways. Amen.

JANUARY 6

> Mine eyes prevent the night watches, that I
> might meditate in thy word. (Psalm 119:148)

As the day ends, you reflect on the happenings of the day. Maybe the day was gloomy but try to find some glimmer of hope from the day. Look at the flowers outside; maybe there is one new flower blooming. It is one small example of God's handiwork.

A rainbow is a glimmer of hope you see after it has rained. You admire the many colors projecting from the rainbow and the size it is in the sky.

God is our ray of hope when life seems unpredictable. Focus on God's promise of eternal life when you experience struggles in your earthly life.

*****

Dear Lord,

Thank you for being my watchful eye in the night. Be with me in my daily struggles and guide me in your pathway. Amen.

JANUARY 7

> But let him ask in faith, nothing wavering.
> For he that wavereth is like a wave of the sea
> driven with the wind and tossed. (James 1:6)

Faith is a strong component in believing in God. God is the one who strengthens your faith. It is by grace you are saved.

There are those who sought out faith in their life. Some of those include Noah, Abraham, and Sarah. They had a strong faith in God that he would deliver them through their journeys.

Do you have a strong faith? If you open your heart, God will strengthen your faith twofold. God is all-powerful and is there for you when you experience difficult times in your life.

Take your concerns to God in prayer. You will be surprised how your life will be enriched while having God in your life.

*****

Dear God,

Thank you for putting faith into my life. Be with me and grant me strength to follow you through my life's journey. Amen.

JANUARY 8

> Finally, brethren, whatsoever things are true, whatsoever things are honest, whatsoever things are just, whatsoever things are pure, whatsoever things are lovely, whatsoever things are of good report; if there be any virtue, and if there be any praise, think on these things. (Philippians 4:8)

People look forward to the future. But if you look back, you will see how you have grown over the past year.

Have confidence in yourself. Be honest with yourself. Be true to yourself. Trust in your actions.

God shows his purity and his loveliness through his Word. Speak highly of the godly virtues you aspire. Living in God's Word through daily Bible reading is justly.

Reflect on oneself, pray, praise, and give thanks. Being worthy of purity puts you in the spirit of Godliness.

*****

Dear God,

Please be with me and protect me as a child of God. Give me the confidence to trust you daily. Amen.

JANUARY 9

> I acknowledged my sin unto thee, and mine iniquity have I not hid. I said, I will confess my transgressions unto the Lord; and thou forgavest the iniquity of my sin. (Psalm 32:5)

Realizing when a sin is committed, we ask for forgiveness. God is always willing to provide forgiveness.

God knows all things; nothing can be hidden. God shows his mercy to everyone, even when sin is evident.

Getting rid of negativity and asking for forgiveness is the first step forward.

The second step would be to "forgive someone else" who may have caused hurt against you. You do not want to carry this grudge with you the rest of your life.

*****

Dear God,

Forgive me for my sin and wrongdoing. Please provide me the strength to be a better Christian. Amen.

JANUARY 10

> These things I have spoken unto you, that in me ye might have peace. In the world ye shall have tribulation: but be of good cheer; I have overcome the world. (John 16:33)

This verse ties in very closely to Philippians 4:7, "And the peace of God, which passeth all understanding, shall keep your hearts and minds through Christ Jesus."

Peace is a calming feeling. Peaceful means restful. When you are at peace with yourself, you are content. There is no controlling in your life.

Only cheerfulness abides in your spirit. To be cheerful and of a free spirit is a good state to be in.

Take time to share your cheerfulness with others this week. Your heart will become full of joy serving others.

*****

Dear God,

Thank you for putting peace into my life. Grant me a willing spirit to turn to you when I need to feel calm and get rid of any stress in my life. Amen.

JANUARY 11

> The fear of the lord is the beginning of knowledge: but fools despise wisdom and instruction. (Proverbs 1:7)

We all know knowledge is powerful. Did you ever stop and think that a new endeavor could change your life?

Your life could change with a simple spiritual download. Reading the Bible every day is very uplifting.

Savor the knowledge you gain from meeting a new friend or attending a church service and taking the sermon message to heart. Instead of shutting down your ego, open up your heart to new insights. God wants you to be knowledgeable in his Word and share it with others.

*****

Dear God,

Thank you for watching over me as I am a sinner. Guide me in the right direction and provide me with the knowledge to bring others to you. Amen.

JANUARY 12

> In the last day, that great day of the feast, Jesus stood and cried, saying, If any man thirst, let him come unto me, and drink. He that believeth on me, as the scripture hath said, out of his belly shall flow rivers of living water. (John 7:37–38)

This verse speaks about the water of life. The river gives life wherever it flows. It also is called a flowing river of blessing, referring to the Holy Spirit. And you shall never thirst if you drink the water.

What a beautiful passage of God's salvation. He gives you everlasting life for believing in Him. Knowing that your thirst is always satisfied is a great reward.

Is your thirst satisfied in the Word of God? Do you need to get more involved in the study of the Bible? It's never too late to start. Do it today. Focusing on one part of the Bible, maybe the New Testament, is a great starting point.

*****

Dear God,

Thank you for providing me the water of life. Grant me your grace to continue down the path of righteousness on my journey to eternal life. Amen.

JANUARY 13

> O how I love thy law! It is my meditation all the day. (Psalm 119:97)

Meditating in God's Word can keep you grounded and focused on your daily living. There are many temptations we experience throughout our life; recognizing the difference between the bad ones and good ones is important. Your thoughts and actions are a reflection of who you are.

Reading the Bible daily will keep you balanced and give you the energy to tackle challenges that come your way.

As you take time to meditate, look at your inward self along with your outward self (how others look at you) and try to find peace and restfulness.

*****

Dear God,

Help me to meditate in your Word every day. Your Word is truly my inspiration for living. Amen.

JANUARY 14

> Thou shalt not avenge, nor bear any grudge against the children of thy people, but thou shalt love thy neighbor as thyself: I am the Lord. (Leviticus 19:18)

Being a good neighbor and showing love and kindness to others is what God wants you to do.

When you see someone in need, ask if they are all right or if they need assistance. Showing you care about their well-being is an encouraging aspect of "being neighborly."

Concentrate on putting others' needs before your own. Look for ways to show unconditional love to others, such as a smile, a hug, or a kind word.

Plan out your day—first by reading the Bible and then interpreting God's Word into loving thoughts throughout the day, and finally analyzing how your day ended up.

*****

Dear God,

Help me to "love my neighbor" every day. Be with me as I show your love to others around me. Amen.

JANUARY 15

> When thou shalt hearken to the voice of the Lord thy God, to keep all his commandments which I command thee this day, to do that which is right in the eyes of the Lord thy God. (Deuteronomy 13:18)

God provides you with the strength and encouragement to keep his commandments. This is not an easy task.

Everyday life presents you with rules to follow, such as at work or at home. Obeying the rules can be a struggle at times. Everyone sins and falls short of expectations. Jesus died on the cross to take away your sins. You have the hope that He overlooks your faults and gives you a clean slate as you start every new day.

Focus on the cross and the significance it represents in your life. God knows your every thought and will guide you in the right direction.

*****

Dear God,

Guide me to obey your commandments in my life. You alone provide the strength and encouragement I need every day. Thank you for being in my life. Amen.

JANUARY 16

> Hide not thy face far from me; put not thy servant away in anger: thou hast been my help; leave me not, neither forsake me, O God of my salvation. (Psalm 27:9)

God is the strength and shield of his people. His heart rejoices and sings praises from above.

God is the almighty protector of every living creature. He looks down from above to make sure harm does not come to his people.

When something bad happens in your life, you may ask, "Why did this happen?" And the answer may be, there was a purpose. We may never know the reason sometimes, but there was probably a lesson to be learned from it. Prayer is the answer when you are troubled in your life. It's a good time for you to talk one-on-one with God for comfort and consolation. Give it a try and see if the result provides you some closure to your concerns.

*****

Dear God,

Thank you for being in my life. Be with me as I follow your path to righteousness. Amen.

JANUARY 17

> But let it be the hidden man of the heart, in that which is not corruptible, even the ornament of a meek and quiet spirit, which is in the sight of God of great price. (1 Peter 3:4)

Have you ever wondered what it would be like to be a king or a queen? Sure, the glamorous life would be nice, but it wouldn't last long. Being a royal has commitments and obligations one must follow for the government.

God has made our beauty on the inside; our ageless beauty is priceless. God instructs us to show our inner beauty to others. Share a hug with a friend or smile at a stranger the next time when you are at the store. The reaction you receive is that love God wants you to share with others.

The more love you share with others, the more fulfilling your life will be.

*****

Dear God,

Thank you for creating the beauty in me. Guide me and protect me as I show your love to others. Amen.

JANUARY 18

> Jesus said unto her, "I am the resurrection, and the life: he that believeth in me, though he were dead, yet shall he live: And whosoever liveth and believeth in me shall never die. Believest thou this?" (John 11:25–26)

What are your beliefs? Do you believe in the resurrection and life? What satisfaction you have if you believe that Jesus gives you life eternal.

Releasing the old beliefs and creating room for the new beliefs or divine wisdom is how God wants you to live your life.

Being open to God's divine wisdom can be as simple as reading the Bible daily or attending a Bible class through the church. God's Word provides you the strength in your life and the encouragement to show love to others.

Believing in God's Word and then living a Godly life provides rich rewards.

*****

Dear God,

Thank you for sending Jesus to die on the cross for me. Give me the strength and wisdom to follow you. Amen.

JANUARY 19

> The Lord is my strength and my shield; my heart trusted in him, and I am helped: therefore my heart greatly rejoiceth; and with my song will I praise him. (Psalm 28:7)

What are your strengths, and what are your weaknesses? Sometimes you dwell on your weaknesses. Instead, you should focus on your strengths and what you can do.

God gives you the strength to overcome your adversities. Make a list of some of your strengths, it could be as simple as: cooking a meal for a shut-in, taking a friend to a doctor appointment or calling a family member you haven't heard from for a while.

Your strengths can be endless, and the gratitude you experience is rewarding. You will realize the many blessings God has showered on you in your life.

*****

Dear God,

Thank you for being my strength and shield. Help me to rejoice and be glad to share your Word with others around me. Amen.

JANUARY 20

> But let him that glorieth glory in this, that he understandeth and knoweth me, that I am the Lord which exercise lovingkindness, judgment, and righteousness, in the earth: for in these things I delight, saith the Lord. (Jeremiah 9:24)

This verse speaks about the Christian maturity with spiritual knowledge and Christlikeness: aiming for a Christian life, conforming to the image of Christ, and reflecting your life as a mirror of the glory of God.

Being perfect like God is impossible. But having faith as simple as a child's will bring you closer to God.

Look up to God and ask for his protection. As you study the Bible, take note how many times love and kindness is recorded. It may surprise you how God emphasizes his love for others.

*****

Dear God,

Thank you for giving me faith in you. Be with me to be more perfect as I study the Bible. Amen.

JANUARY 21

> When I said, My foot slippeth; thy mercy,
> O Lord, held me up. (Psalm 94:18)

Life happens very quickly, and as you get older, the years fly by. First you are in school, then college, maybe get married, start a family, then you are a grandparent. Cherish the memories as life happens around you.

God is your constant; he will be with you when you need Him. God hears your every prayer and loves you every day.

Take your concerns to God in prayer. He will be there to support you along the way. God's unfailing love is your stronghold.

*****

Dear God,

Thank you for your unfailing love. Be with me and guide me to follow your ways as I travel this earth. Amen.

JANUARY 22

> Fear none of those things which thou shalt suffer: behold, the devil shall cast some of you into prison, that ye may be tried; and ye shall have tribulation ten days: be thou faithful unto death, and I will give thee a crown of life. (Revelation 2:10)

Suddenly sharing your faith with others is a powerful tool. You are offered new opportunities daily to proclaim your faith; it could be at work, at your church or when socializing with your friends.

Your spiritual life shows through by your actions or words you use to express yourself. Daily Bible reading helps your spiritual connection with God.

Being faithful to God means taking accountability of your life. Believe in yourself. Encourage others to think positive in their walk with God.

As you become an example of God's handiwork, the rewards you receive will be endless.

*****

Dear God,

Thank you for giving me the promise of eternal life. Grant me peace to serve you in your kingdom until I reach my eternal home in heaven. Amen.

JANUARY 23

> O that thou hadst hearkened to my commandments! Then had thy peace been as a river, and thy righteousness as the waves of the sea.
> (Isaiah 48:18)

Having the peace of God is such a calming feeling. It is like experiencing a divine release of emotions. If you have a task to do, and it's not working out the way you thought it would, try going another avenue. Trying something new may present different opportunities and a whole new perspective.

God knows your thoughts and actions and will encourage you to focus on things you can control, not things out of your control. Letting go of impossible tasks, and going forward with more energy, is just what you may need.

God has asked you to bring your concerns to him in prayer. Prayer is a powerful tool. Taking your burdens to God in prayer means letting go of what you can't control and focusing on truly what you can control in life.

*****

Dear God,

Thank you for giving me peace through times of turmoil. Guide me to take control of my tasks and give the rest of my burdens to you in prayer. Amen.

JANUARY 24

> Let your conversation be without covetousness; and be content with such things as ye have: for he hath said, I will never leave thee, nor forsake thee. (Hebrews 13:5)

God is the Divine Master; he has the highest power. God inspires you to dream big and to take steps in your life you never thought were possible before. Challenge yourself to make a dream into a reality.

If you have often thought of taking a class or a lesson to learn a new task, sign up for the class or lesson today. You may just surprise yourself and enjoy the adventure.

Just remember God is right beside you and he knows your every thought and action.

The new adventure you discovered is enriching your faith. Now God wants you to go out and share his love with others.

*****

Dear God,

Fill me with abundant grace and enrich my faith in you. You are my Divine Master, strengthen me to walk in your ways. Amen.

JANUARY 25

> Be careful for nothing; but in everything by prayer and supplication with thanksgiving let your requests be made known unto God. And the peace of God, which passeth all understanding, shall keep your hearts and minds through Christ Jesus. (Philippians 4:6–7)

We all have a habit of worrying about big and small things. God knows our thoughts and tells us not to be anxious. Take your worries to God in prayer. God will respond to your prayer in the way he sees is best.

Try focusing on positive thoughts. Having a positive outlook on life will help you to learn, grow and challenge yourself. The next time you worry about a task, try to develop a positive outcome of the situation. You may surprise yourself. Approach every situation with a chance to explore your horizons, and God will be at your side every step of the way.

*****

Dear God,

Thank you for sending Jesus to take away my sins. Be with me and guide me as I venture through life. You alone are my shepherd. Amen.

JANUARY 26

> The Lord is nigh unto all them that call
> upon him, to all that call upon him in truth.
> (Psalm 145:18)

God wants you to be courageous and brave. Do not be afraid of your enemies but instead put on the armor of bravery.

You are worthy of God's grace and wisdom. Every day God shows His abundance to you through your coworkers, your family, or your friends. Take time to actually *listen* to what people are saying to you. Listening closely to the words in a song is a good example. Those words can be a direct hit to your heart and show you just how special people are to you in your life.

God wants you to call upon Him in your time of need. He listens to your prayers. Your prayers may not be answered the way you want them to be answered, but God does always answer your prayers.

It's a tough subject; so try to imagine if you could be God for one day. Would your reaction be any different? God's blessings.

*****

Dear God,

Make me worthy of your grace and wisdom. Guide me to follow you for a faith-based life. Amen.

JANUARY 27

> If any of you lack wisdom, let him ask of God,
> that giveth to all men liberally, and upbraideth
> not; and it shall be given him. (James 1:5)

The source of wisdom comes from asking God in prayer for the gift of wisdom. Wisdom comes from God. It may be promised from above.

God gives in superabundant measures to his people. An example would be feeding the five thousand on only two loaves of bread. He makes sure you are filled up with what you need for your daily needs.

So the next time you are in need of some wisdom, ask God to shine down on you and spread some of his gifts upon you. You may be surprised at his response and the gifts he may provide to you. God's blessings.

*****

Dear God,

Thank you for giving me wisdom and understanding. Only you can know how I feel in my life. Be with me and guide me to follow the path you have laid out for me in my life. Amen.

JANUARY 28

> Let the words of my mouth, and the meditation of my heart, be acceptable in thy sight, O Lord, my strength, and my redeemer. (Psalm 19:14)

This verse speaks about various "wise words" relating to this passage, including *forcible, pleasant, appropriate, gracious, inspiring, unforgettable,* and *comforting*. Quite a variety of emotions for this meditation.

When reading the Bible, you may come across specific words which emit emotions you may feel about a situation. It's okay to have feelings. God made everyone with different personalities; no two people are alike.

God made you unique or special. Take time out of your busy day to meditate and talk to God about some of your "wise thoughts" you have. It will put peace and calm into your life.

Just be patient, and God will guide you on how to handle the situation. God is a patient God and knows the struggle His people face when circumstances are difficult to handle. It will all work out in the long run. God's blessings.

Dear God,

Thank you for putting wise words into my life. Be gracious unto me and grant me wisdom to know and do your will. Amen.

JANUARY 29

> And that from a child thou hast known the holy scriptures, which are able to make thee wise unto salvation through faith which is in Christ Jesus. All scripture is given by inspiration of God, and is profitable for doctrine, for reproof, for correction, for instruction in righteousness: That the man of God may be perfect, thoroughly furnished unto all good works. (2 Timothy 3:15–17)

These verses speak of the value of scriptures. We learn from God youthful piety, children instruction, His Word as a light, wisdom, salvation, saving faith, perfection, spiritual preparation along with good works.

Oh, to have all these values or even just a few of them in your life. Take the time to research some of these values in your Bible. They can be life-changing and inspire you to share God's Word with others around you.

*****

Dear God,

Thank you for providing me the values of the scriptures. Grant me grace to know you better and tell others of your saving grace. Amen.

JANUARY 30

> But my God shall supply all your need according to his riches in glory by Christ Jesus. (Philippians 4:19)

Sometimes children of God get their wants and needs mixed up. God provides for the needs for his children. The wants of his children can get in the way of God's love for you. God provides you with unconditional love and will always be there for you, especially when you have trials and tribulations.

When you are faced with a medical condition, and it looks bleak, take it to God in prayer to ask for his guidance.

God is all-knowing and will strengthen your faith to cope with any adversity you are facing. Don't give up on God; he does not give up on you.

If you have a Bible, open it and start reading some of your favorite or familiar passages. It is sure to enlighten your spirit and bring joy to your reading.

Try sharing a couple of the passages with your family and see if they also have a favorite verse. God is truly working in you and will be there on your journey to eternal life.

*****

Dear God,

Be with me as I try to decipher between wants and needs. Guide me down the pathway of life you would choose for me. Amen.

JANUARY 31

> Set a watch, O Lord, before my mouth;
> keep the door of my lips. (Psalm 141:3)

There are two parts to this verse. Divine restraint tells you to forgive those indebted to you. And you should ask God to put his hand over you to protect you from evil.

The second part of the verse is the tongue restraints. Keeping your tongue from speaking evil. If you curb your tongue, then you shall keep your life.

It's a hard thing to do, especially when the devil is tempting you to speak unkindly about people.

As Proverbs 21:23 says, "Whoso keepeth his mouth and his tongue, keepeth his soul from troubles."

Ask God to curb your tongue, so you can control your language. God is all-powerful and can work wonders on his people. Give God a chance in your life. God's blessings.

*****

Dear God,

Thank you for being my Divine Restraint. Keep me controlled on my journey to eternal life. Amen.

FEBRUARY 1

> Thou hast also given me the shield of thy salvation: and thy right hand hath holden me up, and thy gentleness hath made me great. (Psalm 18:35)

God's protection is all around you. God surrounds you and answers your prayers. Look around you; when you are struggling with an issue, God gives you the light to keep going up. Look to God's love for that hope of salvation. He died on the cross to forgive your sins.

God protects you from every kind of evil. He is always there when you need his assistance.

And when you do make wrong choices in life, remember God is by your side—you have nothing to fear.

*****

Dear God,

Thank you for being my protector from harm and danger. Be with me when I am faced with choices to make in life. Give me the strength to make the right decision. Amen.

FEBRUARY 2

> And all things, whatsoever ye shall ask in prayer, believing, ye shall receive. (Matthew 21:22)

Have you ever asked God for something in prayer? Did he answer your prayer? Did the outcome surprise you?

Believing in yourself, not comparing yourself to someone else, is the key to self-confidence. Practice standing your ground and believe anything is possible on your journey through life.

God knows your every thought and will grant you his peace when the time is right. You may wish for a happy outcome, but God may change the path and provide an unlikely result. The outcome may make you stop and think, "Why did this happen?" Only God knows the answer.

Simply take your prayer request to God and believe. He will respond. You will receive an answer…but be satisfied with the outcome. God alone has the vision of what he wants for you. Trust in his power.

*****

Dear God,

Thank you for believing in me. Grant me your grace to live your Word through your Bible teachings. Amen.

FEBRUARY 3

> If we confess our sins, he is faithful and just to forgive us our sins, and to cleanse us from all unrighteousness. (1 John 1:9)

Do you take responsibility for your actions? In the same way, we must confess our sins to God. He will forgive our wrongdoings and give us a clean slate. How wonderful is that!

Reflecting on your inner growth when you sin shows you are determined to take ownership of your actions. Your inner growth is made by the choices you make on a daily basis. You may choose to show kindness today or choose to help a friend with an errand. For everything you do in life—choose wisely.

As you sin daily, God wants you to be accountable for your sins; but remember, he will forgive you, as he is all-powerful.

Take time today to reflect on your inner growth and thank him for your existence.

*****

Dear God,

Great is your faithfulness. Thank you for forgiving my sins when I do wrong. Guide me down the path to reach your heavenly splendor in heaven someday. Amen.

FEBRUARY 4

> Draw nigh to God, and he will draw nigh to you. Cleanse your hands, ye sinners; and purify your hearts, ye double minded. (James 4:8)

Look to the heavens and to God as he is the all-knowing and all-powerful one. God knows your every thought and action.

As you go through life, you are faced with various relationships and opportunities. Choosing the correct one may change the course your life is going. Always look to God for his direction.

Reading the Bible daily is a good first step as you draw yourself to God. God knows you are capable of great things; look to the scriptures for guidance.

*****

Dear God,

Thank you for guiding me through your scriptures. As I draw nigh to you, be with me to take the right path that leads to you. Amen.

FEBRUARY 5

> Let us not be desirous of vain glory, provoking one another, envying one another. (Galatians 5:26)

Do you ever feel jealous of what others have? You may feel low self-esteem at times. God wants you to stay focused on the blessings and good fortune you have in your life.

Singing in church may be what you like to do. Maybe your voice doesn't qualify you to be in the choir, but you can still sing the songs from your heart. You may live in a small house but be grateful you have a house. A bigger house isn't always what a person needs; it just comes with more maintenance and cleaning.

Feel your joy within you, the love that God shines down upon you. God loves you just the way you are. Just accept his grace and live your life as if there is no tomorrow.

*****

Dear God,

Thank you for making me just as I am. Guide me and protect me in your faith so I can share your Word with others. Amen.

FEBRUARY 6

> O give thanks unto the Lord; for he is good:
> for his mercy endureth forever. (Psalm 136:1)

This is a powerful prayer. You should stop and think about the words, saying the prayer slowly. Thank God for the meal you are about to partake of and realize where the food came from, such as a garden or a farmer's field.

God's mercy endures forever and all he asks of you is to thank him daily, especially before a meal.

Thank God daily for everything in your life; it could be for household chores or other small tasks you do without realizing that God provides for your daily living.

You should practice gratitude for your daily tasks even though you do them without thanking God. He alone is your strength and provider.

*****

Dear God,

I give you my thanks and praise for providing me with everything I need for my daily living. Be with me and strengthen my faith through your scriptures. Amen.

FEBRUARY 7

> And why take ye thought for raiment? Consider the lilies of the field, how they grow; they toil not, neither do they spin: And yet I say unto you, That even Solomon in all his glory was not arrayed like one of these. (Matthew 6:28–29)

Growth relates to change. Flowers start out as a seed, then are fertilized, and then watered into blooming flowers. Life also has constant change. Just when you think life is stable and predictable, the inevitable happens. Change. Change is all around us.

God gave us the Bible, which has been around forever. God's Word does not change but provides constant strength and peace. Embrace change in your life, but plant yourself on God's firm foundation.

*****

Dear God,

Thank you for providing change in my life. Help me to embrace an ever-changing world and look to you for my inner strength. Amen.

FEBRUARY 8

> Humble yourselves in the sight of the Lord,
> and he shall lift you up. (James 4:10)

Being humble may be a difficult task. You may be giving up something you really enjoy doing or parting with a favorite item.

God wants you to be humble but also then reach for the unknown. Your happiness depends on venturing out and learning new tasks or meeting new people. God wants what's best for you. He knows your potential. Next time you experience an uneasy task, say a prayer and ask God to guide you in the right direction. You will amaze yourself. The challenge of experiencing a new adventure is exhilarating. Just try it.

*****

Dear God,

Thank you for teaching me to be humble. Your guidance and direction will take me to new levels in my spiritual path. Amen.

FEBRUARY 9

> The grass withereth, the flower fadeth: but the word of our God shall stand for ever. (Isaiah 40:8)

Wherever you go, people are encouraging you to read the Bible. Do they realize you studied God's Word in school, in Bible class, and in church every Sunday. Does it ever end? No, God wants you to be studious and live by the Bible teachings.

God sent his Son to take away your sins. God's blessings are showered upon you by his love for you. You can be assured he protects you from harm and danger every day.

If you are ever afraid, take your concern to God in prayer, and he will give you the confidence to tackle your concern. Just trust in God for guidance.

*****

Dear God,

Thank you for giving me the Bible. It is my instruction book for living my life. Grant me your protection and strength to follow your path in life. Amen.

FEBRUARY 10

> But they that wait upon the Lord shall renew their strength; they shall mount up with wings as eagles; they shall run, and not be weary; and they shall walk, and not faint. (Isaiah 40:31)

Are you ever scared and not sure which direction to turn? You should never feel alone. God is always with you. He knows your every thought and action.

You are unique and God wants you to embrace your individuality. Stay focused on yourself. Take one step at a time and you will eventually come to terms with your strength. On your journey through life, take time to dream of the future: your lifestyle, your family, or your job. Where do you think you will be in five years or ten years? Don't hold back on your dreams. They may just become reality someday.

God will be beside you on your journey through life. He will give you the strength to get through every day. He is listening to you wherever you are.

*****

Dear God,

Thank you for giving me strength and keeping me secure on my journey through life. Be with me and protect me while I share your gospel with others. Amen.

FEBRUARY 11

> In all thy ways acknowledge him, and he
> shall direct thy paths. (Proverbs 3:6)

You are faced with many choices to make on a daily basis. Choosing the correct path is critical.

Using the Bible as your guidebook, you can read various stories of triumphs or adversities. The options for reading the Bible come in a variety of forms: on the computer, in book form, or on your phone.

God knows exactly what a person needs throughout the day. His Word will inspire you to be a better person and to become more positive in your life.

Making the choice to open your Bible and start reading chapter by chapter is a good start. If that is not an option, then try to find your favorite Bible verses that you may have marked in your Bible in the past. The possibilities are endless.

*****

Dear God,

Thank you for giving me the Bible. Guide me as I begin my journey in studying your Word more faithfully. Amen.

FEBRUARY 12

> I will praise thee; for I am fearfully and
> wonderfully made: marvelous are thy works; and
> that my soul knoweth right well. (Psalm 139:14)

God made you unique. Every person was created with a purpose. If you don't know your purpose in life, stay tuned; God will reveal it to you. As mentioned in the text, "Fearfully and wonderfully made." What a beautiful reference for you.

No two people are alike, including twins. They may seem similar, but small differences make each one unique.

So true is the Bible. Jesus has many comparisons in the Bible of stories of his love and compassion. Each story has a purpose and a lesson learned.

You are a God's treasure. Use your time wisely and listen to what God is providing you in his Word. It will change your life.

*****

Dear God,

Thank you for giving me the Bible to study your Word. Be with me and grant me your peace while I am on your path of righteousness. Amen.

FEBRUARY 13

> Be kindly affectioned one to another with brotherly love; in honor preferring one another; Not slothful in business; fer-vent in spirit; serving the Lord; Rejoicing in hope; patient in tribulation; continuing instant in prayer; Distributing to the necessity of saints; given to hospitality. (Romans 12:10–13)

What beautiful words from scripture. True words to live by.

Love—you want genuine love from your family and friends. In turn, you should pass on that love to others.

Serve—serve the Lord with your heart and enthusiastically to honor him.

Rejoice—or praise the Lord with songs of delightfulness.

Confident hope—a guarantee of hope from God for a future home in heaven.

Patience—remaining calm when troubles surround you.

Praying—pray without ceasing. Prayers work wonders. Never give up on praying.

Help—helping others in time of need. Showing compassion to others without expecting anything in return.

*****

Dear God,

Thank you for the Bible and your precious Words to live by. Be with me as I follow your path to heaven. Amen.

FEBRUARY 14

> For I am persuaded, that neither death, nor life, nor angels, nor principalities, nor powers, nor things present, nor things to come, Nor height, nor depth, nor any other creature, shall be able to separate us from the love of God, which is in Christ Jesus our Lord. (Romans 8:38–39)

God's love is like finding joy in your life. Embracing every moment and experiencing the feeling of joy is what love is all about. It could be as simple as a walk in the park, enjoying the morning sunrise or hearing the birds chirping. Taking in nature is a beautiful reflection of God's handiwork.

God cares about you and adores you. He knows your every thought and action. As you go through life, stop and think of the many blessings God has provided for you. He has granted you with a loving family and friends around you to share special times with.

The next time you question God's love for you, look at the treasures he has bestowed on you and the beauty in his creation.

*****

Dear God,

Thank you for loving me and sending Jesus to die on the cross to take away my sin. Be with me on my journey to eternal life. Amen.

FEBRUARY 15

> For we are his workmanship, created in Christ Jesus unto good works, which God hath before ordained that we should walk in them. (Ephesians 2:10)

You are considered God's workmanship; he is the Master creator. God doesn't make mistakes. He is perfect. As you go through life, you want life to be perfect, but that doesn't always happen. You mess up and then need to ask God for forgiveness.

You are unique, even though you have flaws. God created everyone with unique characteristics, such as tall, short, different skin color, or different hair color.

You are truly special in God's eyes. God made you the way you are. Embrace your beauty and thank God for his workmanship. It is his gift to you.

*****

Dear God,

Thank you for your workmanship. You are the Master of the universe. Thank you for your creation and the beauty of those around us. Amen.

FEBRUARY 16

> And we know that all things work together for good to them that love God, to them who are the called according to his purpose. (Romans 8:28)

Have you ever been inspired to go somewhere or do a particular task? People or events inspire you to seek adventure. God has a purpose for you on this earth. He wants you to look around to take in all his creation. Be inspired.

Pursue a new passion on your journey; volunteer at the theatre, visit an art museum, or find a new book to read. Challenge yourself to try a new adventure. Embrace your energy and explore God's creation.

*****

Dear God,

Thank you for giving me purpose on this earth. Guide me and protect me as I make my journey through this life. Amen.

FEBRUARY 17

> For as the sufferings of Christ abound in us, so our consolation also aboundeth by Christ. (2 Corinthians 1:5)

Do you ever need comforting if you have had a bad day? Everyone has a bad day sometimes; do not dwell on it.

God is there with his abundance of mercy to shower you with his love. He sent Jesus to die on the cross to take away your sins. God is truly amazing. He understands your hurt, since he has been there in the past.

When you experience life's trials and tribulations, try going to scripture and see what God recommends for a solution.

God's comforting words in the Bible may be just the answer to your prayers. God's love is abundant, and there is plenty of love for your entire life. Take the journey with God at your side and enjoy the ride.

*****

Dear God,

Thank you for your abundant love showered on me. Be with me on my life's journey as I study your word. Amen.

FEBRUARY 18

> Rejoice in the Lord always; and again I say, Rejoice. (Philippians 4:4)

As you think about rejoicing, you may want to ponder your good fortune you have received in your life: your friendships you have established, the kind words people have said to you, or the opportunities to serve either at your church or with an organization.

Showing your gratitude to others is so rewarding. You can reap the benefits your entire life. Consider the many blessings God has bestowed on you. It is your job now to praise his name and share His Gospel with others.

Your task in life is to go and "tell it on the mountain" to anyone who will listen. Singing in a choir and partaking in a Bible class are just a few examples of spreading God's Word. You are God's ambassador; use your time wisely.

*****

Dear God,

Thank you for sending Jesus to take away my sins. Use me as your ambassador to spread your Word to others in your kingdom. Amen.

FEBRUARY 19

> And this is the confidence that we have in him, that, if we ask any thing according to his will, he heareth us. (1 John 5:14)

Do you have confidence in God? He has confidence in you. He hears everything you say, and he knows your thoughts.

What is your communication with family and friends? Is it text, email, or verbal conversation? A lot of communication has changed over the years. With the changing times comes changing communication. You need to adjust your communication to be in touch with reality.

This is also true in our communication with God. When we ask God for a request through prayer, be confident and wait patiently for an answer. The answer may not be what you were expecting, but God decides the response. Be patient and understanding; the response is from God.

*****

Dear God,

Thank you for having confidence in me. Please grant me patience as I do your will and spread your gospel to others. Amen.

FEBRUARY 20

> Charity suffereth long and is kind; charity envieth not; charity vaunteth not itself, is not puffed up, Doth not behave itself unseemly, seeketh not her own, is not easily provoked, thinketh no evil. (1 Corinthians 13:4–5)

Love makes the world go round, or so they say. God wants you to show love to others just as he loves you.

Along with love comes patience and kindness. Listening to others' concerns is one example of being patient. Showing kindness takes a very patient person, especially understanding the person's well-being and then spreading kindness to them with a simple smile or compliment to them.

God encourages you to choose your words wisely and not be unkind to others. Use a soft tongue if others treat you badly. Using a kind gesture is a better example for communication.

*****

Dear God,

Help me to be patient and kind to others. Be with me as I show love to others in your kingdom. Amen.

FEBRUARY 21

We love him, because he first loved us. (1 John 4:19)

What is love in action? How do you show love to others? Some examples may be:

1. Making someone feel special with a card saying, "Thinking of you."
2. Listen to someone very carefully and thoughtfully with an attentive ear and acknowledging what they said to you.
3. Keep a promise you made to someone like cleaning their house or mowing the lawn.

These gestures of love show your concern and show others your love.

Life is too short, so start showing love to others today. Tomorrow may be too late.

Make a list of love attributes you can do for others, and you will be surprised how long your list will become. God loves you and wants you to share that love with others.

*****

Dear God,

Thank you for loving me unconditionally. Guide and protect me to show your love to others in your kingdom. Amen.

FEBRUARY 22

> For the grace of God that bringeth salvation hath appeared to all men, Teaching us that, denying ungodliness and worldly lusts, we should live soberly, righteously, and godly, in this present world. (Titus 2:11–12)

God's gifts to us are his saving grace, his saving faith and the salvation which is given to everyone who believes. These gifts are given to you out of love and compassion.

Parents provide for their children because they love them. Parents sacrifice raising their children, so their children have the best while growing up.

God looks down from heaven and wants the best for you also. He knows the most beautiful things in the world cannot be seen or even touched but felt within your heart. God's blessings.

*****

Dear God,

Thank you for providing your grace and salvation to me. Be with me as I go out into the world and share your gospel with others. Amen.

FEBRUARY 23

> For the wages of sin is death; but the gift of
> God is eternal life through Jesus Christ our Lord.
> (Romans 6:23)

The ultimate sacrifice was made by Jesus. He died on the cross to take away your sins. Your sins are now forgiven. What a marvelous gift for you.

God's overflowing love for you connects you with everlasting gratitude. As you feel the uplifting of emotions flow through your mind, stop and visualize the value of God's love. Visualizing the earthly surroundings of nature, and God's creation is marvelous. A walk in the park, hearing the birds sing, and noticing the wildflowers in bloom are just a few of the wonders in this universe.

Learning to appreciate the blessings God has bestowed on you can fill your soul with his free gift to you.

*****

Dear God,

Thank you for giving me the wages of sin for death. I am now free from Satan's wrath. Be with me to go forward and spread your gospel to others. Amen.

FEBRUARY 24

> O Lord, thou hast searched me, and known me. Thou knowest my downsitting and mine uprising, thou understandest my thought afar off. Thou compassest my path and my lying down, and art acquainted with all my ways. For there is not a word in my tongue, but, lo, O Lord, thou knowest it altogether. (Psalm 139:1–4)

God is all-knowing or omniscient. David praises God for his all-seeing providence. God's knowledge is divine. He revealeth the deep and secret things. He knoweth what is in the darkness and what is in the light. God knows what things you have need of before you even ask for them.

What a powerful God. There are probably a lot of things you don't know about yourself, but God does.

Take your concerns to God in prayer. You may be surprised at the response you receive. God does want the best for you. Give him a chance to show you how to put joy in your life.

*****

Dear God,

Thank you for being all-powerful to me on this earth. Guide me and protect me to follow your path to righteousness. Amen.

FEBRUARY 25

> Now are we sure that thou knowest all things, and needest not that any man should ask thee: by this we believe that thou camest forth from God. (John 16:30)

Connecting to divine intervention is up to you. God provides the tools and then lets the mind, body, and spirit unite. If you have ever gone to a spa, you will recognize the tranquility you receive. It's uplifting.

Meditation has a calming effect when you let God take control of your body and mind. Put God in control and then sit back and enjoy the ride.

Early morning is a good time to meditate, since every day is a new day. Take your prayer requests to God and then wait for his response. God is truly in control of your life.

*****

Dear God,

Thank you for your divine intervention in my life. Guide me to serve you and do more meditation in my prayer life. Amen.

FEBRUARY 26

>And if I go and prepare a place for you, I will come again, and receive you unto myself; that where I am, there ye may be also. (John 14:3)

What an inspiring scripture. Jesus died on the cross to take away your sins. You can be assured your salvation is won.

In similarity, you are renewing yourself. Letting God take over your life, and he is now the focus of your life. Giving your life to God, every day every moment, and looking to him to start your new life.

Keeping the faith when times get tough can be a real challenge. Stay focused on the Bible, maybe write down one to two of your favorite Bible verses to focus on every week. The inspiration a Bible verse provides is simply amazing. God's blessings.

*****

Dear God,

Thank you for sending Jesus to die on the cross for me. Be with me as I challenge myself to read the Bible more and share my life with others. Amen.

FEBRUARY 27

> The eyes of your understanding being enlightened; that ye may know what is the hope of his calling and what the riches of the glory of his inheritance in the saints. (Ephesians 1:18)

Enlightenment may be similar to personal wisdom. Be proud of what you have accomplished in your spiritual life. Share your religious background with others; it could be as simple as in a grocery store by saying, "God bless you."

While sitting in a hospital waiting room, you may see a person alone with a concerned look. Ask the person if you can pray for them or their loved one. Prayer has an impact on people, and you may be just the answer they needed at that time in their life.

Be bold in your faith and don't be afraid to share it with others. God will guide you in your faith, just follow his lead.

*****

Dear God,

Thank you for enlightening me in your Word. Guide me in my faith so I may be an example to others in sharing your gospel. Amen.

FEBRUARY 28

> Then said Jesus to those Jews which believed on him, If ye continue in my word, then are ye my disciples indeed; And ye shall know the truth, and the truth shall make you free. (John 8:31–32)

Follow your passion in life. As Jesus said to his disciples, "Remain faithful." When you have a passion, you are inspired to tell others so that they may like to do it also. So true is a passion for attending a special event. You want to tell others the enjoyment you received while attending and proud of the performers.

Jesus wants you to be passionate about his teachings, the Bible, and to tell others. Sharing your faith day by day is an enlightening experience, and the joy you feel will light up your world.

*****

Dear God,

Thank you for teaching me through your disciples. Make me an example of your faithfulness to share your gospel with others. Amen.

MARCH 1

> For I know the thoughts that I think toward you, saith the Lord, thoughts of peace, and not of evil, to give you an expected end. (Jeremiah 29:11)

What are your plans for the future? You may not know your plans, but God does. When you were younger, you probably dreamed of being like a favorite actor or someone prominent in your family or community.

And then as the years went by, you were closer to college age and realized you needed to make a more logical decision of what you wanted to do in life as a career or what college you wanted to attend.

It was your time to speak up, and with a confident voice, your opinion was expressed. Your choices in life were evident, and you turned to others around you for advice.

God put his loving arms around you. Your future is still in the works, but now God is your captain and steers the boat in the direction of eternal life. Follow his plan and see what path you take to righteousness.

*****

Dear God,

Thank you for planning out my future for me. You alone are my guide and know what path to be on. Amen.

MARCH 2

> Now the God of hope fill you with all joy and peace in believing, that ye may abound in hope, through the power of the Holy Ghost. (Romans 15:13)

You have probably heard of the song, "Joy, joy, joy, joy in my heart, joy in my heart for you…" What an inspiring verse to think God wants us to be joyful and happy all the time. We know it's not always possible, but it keeps you positive.

You should appreciate the many blessings God has provided you on a daily basis—your health, your family, and your friends.

Take time today to thank a friend for their unconditional love; the gesture will amaze you. You may also want to show some self-care to yourself by going to a park for a walk or going to the library and checking out a book on one of your favorite subjects. Explore new adventures in your life.

*****

Dear God,

Thank you for putting joy in my life. Be with me on my journey through life to show more joy to others I meet. Amen.

MARCH 3

> For he satisfieth the longing soul, and filleth
> the hungry soul with goodness. (Psalm 107:9)

Embrace your strengths and weaknesses in your life. Be aware of how you conduct yourself around others. Sometimes your actions speak louder than your words. God does satisfy you with good things, and you may just need to wait for them. As a Christian, you should seek His Word. Are you hungry for the Bible? Scripture has many examples of food as they relate to food for the soul. One story is the feeding of the five thousand using a simple loaf of bread and how it multiplied to feed the multitude of people.

God wants you to share His Word with others. It can simply be a kind gesture or a smile to show you care for others. Be bold and share your life with others today.

Take time to set aside a special time for you and God to spend time together. It will be well worth the effort you put forth.

*****

Dear God,

Thank you for satisfying my thirsty needs for your work. Be with me and guide me to share Your Word with others. Amen.

MARCH 4

> A new commandment I give unto you, that ye love one another; as I have loved you, that ye also love one another. By this shall all men know that ye are my disciples, if ye have love one to another. (John 13:34–35)

At the Last Supper, Jesus gave the command to the disciples. It's not as easy as it sounds.

Do you love your family and friends? Do you have one member of your family that love may be compromised? No family is perfect. God understands the circumstances, and it can be a difficult situation at times.

Treating others with kindness and respect is sometimes a trying task. Knowing you are a Christian, look for opportunities to remedy the solution.

Start with your actions and take one day at a time. Putting your best foot forward to show love to others is what God would want you to do.

*****

Dear God,

Thank you for giving the command to love one another. It is not an easy task to do as a sinner. Be with me and show me the way to your salvation. Amen.

MARCH 5

> Be not deceived; God is not mocked: for whatsoever a man soweth, that shall he also reap. For he that soweth to his flesh shall of the flesh reap corruption; but he that soweth to the Spirit shall of the Spirit reap life everlasting. (Galatians 6:7–8)

If you have ever had a garden, then you know it requires seeds, some digging in the dirt, some water, and then sun to make the seeds grow. Over a few weeks, the beauty of the garden grows, and God's creation is revealed. After the plants have grown, it is then time to harvest the garden and enjoy the food.

God has planted us on this earth to flourish and tell others of his love. So like a garden, you grow in His Word and bloom where you are planted.

*****

Dear God,

Thank you for planting me on this earth. Guide me as I share your garden of love with others. Amen.

MARCH 6

> Which hope we have as an anchor of the
> soul, both sure and steadfast, and which entereth
> into that within the veil. (Hebrews 6:19)

Hope can be compared to a ship; you need the anchor to keep you secure and stable in water. Without an anchor, a ship would be wandering at sea.

So true in life, you need God's hope to keep you grounded in His Word. If you are going through a difficult time in life, you need to take care of yourself. Put energy into your self-care. Focus on one aspect of your life and try to improve it one day at a time.

God is considered the anchor of the soul. He offers you His hope. You can lean on Him when you are weary and heavy laden, and He will guide you to still waters. The next time you are lost and feel hopeless, pray to God for guidance to get you through; He will be there to take care of you.

*****

Dear God,

Thank you for being my hope in troubling waters. Guide me to still waters so that I may have the hope of eternal life. Amen.

MARCH 7

> Give unto the Lord the glory due unto his name; worship the Lord in the beauty of holiness. (Psalm 29:2)

Giving God the glory is the same as praising God. Do you give those around you praise for doing a good job? Everyone loves when they receive a compliment. It simply boosts their spirit and makes you feel good.

Giving someone a compliment when they least expect it is what God wants you to do. Sharing His love with others grows Christianity in His kingdom.

Attending church on a regular basis allows you to sing his praises and fill up with the gospel every week. As the words say, "Go out and make disciples of all nations," spreading God's Word to everyone around you. God wants you to be living what the gospel teaches and showing warmth and joy to others.

*****

Dear God,

Thank you for providing joy in my life. Teach me to share your warmth and joy to others. Amen.

MARCH 8

> Teaching them to observe all things whatsoever I have commanded you: and, lo, I am with you always, even unto the end of the world. (Matthew 28:20)

As a child, when you were with your parents, did you ever try to stray away from them, because you were curious and wanted to see what was going on? You were probably scolded and told to stay by their side.

You may have strayed away from God when he gives you instructions to follow him. Going to church every Sunday to hear His Word is what he asks of you, but sometimes you were tempted by the devil and stayed home from church to sleep in.

God knows your every thought and action. He wants you to follow his command and follow him. The next time you are tempted by the devil, step back and think about everything God has done for you. You will be glad you had the time to think about your decision.

*****

Dear God,

Thank you for being with me always. I may try to lead but will need your guidance to keep me on the right path. Amen.

MARCH 9

> And the Lord God planted a garden eastward in Eden; and there he put the man whom he had formed. (Genesis 2:8)

A garden is both beautiful and cumbersome to take care of. A garden requires weeding, watering, fertilizing, and harvesting the vegetables.

In God's garden of life, he provides you with the Bible as your garden. Your task is to read the scriptures and live by them. There could be weeds (or sins) along the way that may need to be fertilized (by heeding His Word).

You may feel uncomfortable with listening to God's Word but instead take the time to grow your spiritual life as God is shaping you for His kingdom. He is asking for your patience and understanding while studying His Word. Take the time to enjoy your garden of life.

*****

Dear God,

Thank you for including me in your garden of life. Be with me and protect me as I walk in your ways to your pathway to heaven. Amen.

MARCH 10

> But even the very hairs of your head are all numbered. Fear not therefore: ye are of more value than many sparrows. (Luke 12:7)

The hairs on your head are numbered. God created you special and knows your thoughts and actions. God knows each part of you, from the color of your eyes to what you will be when you grow up. God is all-knowing.

God provides you with wisdom and emotions so you can focus your energy on living a godly life. Everyone sins and falls short of the glory of God. But thanks be to God your sins are forgiven and salvation awaits you.

Treat each day as a new day in God's kingdom. You were set free and can now go and share His Word with others. Go and tell it on the mountain…to all who will hear His Word.

*****

Dear God,

Thank you for creating me in your image. Be with me and guide me through life's struggles to share your Word with others around me. Amen.

MARCH 11

> Search me, O God, and know my heart: try me, and know my thoughts: And see if there be any wicked way in me and lead me in the way everlasting. (Psalm 139:23–24)

Do you practice discipline or self-control? Do not be anxious about your life. God controls your thoughts and actions and in due time will make them come to pass.

Life may be difficult at times; please be patient with God. He will give you the inner strength and growth to tackle obstacles you are facing on a daily basis.

Go to God in prayer and supplication knowing he will help you demonstrate the clear path to take in your life.

Take some time today and give some extra assistance to someone who could use your help. You will be glad you did. Your kindness does not go unnoticed.

*****

Dear God,

Thank you for sending Jesus to take away my sins. Guide me in my prayer life so I may be with you in heaven someday. Amen.

MARCH 12

> Let him that stole steal no more: but rather let him labor, working with his hands the thing which is good, that he may have to give to him that needeth. (Ephesians 4:28)

Being generous is related to giving. You give of yourself to others. Giving of your time or giving of your talents is what God instructs you to do.

When an event occurs at your church or in your community, it takes time to set up, work the event, and also clean up. In addition, you may be asked to donate food or materials for the event. The word is *volunteer* (or serve). Many hands helping at an event make the workload lighter.

The next time you are asked to help at an event, consider compassion and sharing what you have been blessed with, and then answer, "*Yes*, I would love to help."

The satisfaction of knowing you took an interest in someone else is so rewarding.

*****

Dear God,

Thank you for showing me the importance of generosity. Be with me as I show compassion to others in the future. Amen.

MARCH 13

> But he, being full of the Holy Ghost, looked up steadfastly into heaven, and saw the glory of God, and Jesus standing on the right hand of God. (Acts 7:55)

This verse talks about heaven. Christ is the Great Counselor. He comforts his people, goes to prepare a heavenly home for those who seek him, and then ascends into heaven.

God is waiting for you when your time is at hand. Are you prepared to enter heaven? May be something to think about. Do you have your affairs in order?

You may think you have plenty of time on this earth. Some people are taken to heaven way too quickly and are sometimes not prepared.

Take life one day at a time and make the best of every day, as it could be your last. Ask God to give you peace and understanding to prepare your life for heaven someday.

*****

Dear God,

Thank you for giving me the opportunity to go to heaven someday. Please give me peace and understanding so I can prepare my life for eternal life. Amen.

MARCH 14

> Desiring to be teachers of the law; understanding neither what they say, nor whereof they affirm. (1 Timothy 1:7)

This verse talks about the contentious Spirit or man who kindles his strife. The verse also talks about false teachers who teach things they ought not, such as filthy or corrupt actions. And the third part of this verse is about spiritual ignorance or not obeying God's righteousness.

Have you ever been in a contentious state of mind? Maybe not sure if what you were doing was the right thing to do? Have a conversation with God and ask for guidance and understanding.

*****

Dear God,

Thank you for calming my contentious strife in life. Guide me to make better decisions with my life and follow your example. Amen.

MARCH 15

> The Lord shall preserve thy going out and thy coming in from this time forth, and even for evermore. (Psalm 121:8)

Are you an adventurous person? Do you like new experiences to try? Having a mindset of adventure does have consequences. The fear of getting hurt or the fear of failing the task. God knows your every thought and action. God knows if you will be successful or unsuccessful.

Everyone makes mistakes, and that helps you overcome the ability to get up from your mistakes and tackle it again.

God wants you to be confident about your actions and be willing to explore new avenues. God will give you the strength needed to be successful in your task.

*****

Dear God,

Thank you for watching over me when I am adventurous. Be with me as I tackle new adventures in the future. Amen.

MARCH 16

> And the grace of our Lord was exceeding abundant with faith and love which is in Christ Jesus. (1 Timothy 1:14)

Do you ever get tempted by all the commercials, billboards, or Facebook to buy things you don't really need? You get tempted by the devil to have the most up-to-date phones, clothes, gadgets, and the list goes on.

God doesn't want you to get caught up in the worldly things but stay focused on the Bible and its teachings. God will provide for you. Reading the Bible will provide you with all the riches you will ever need.

God shares his grace with you daily. Start each day with the Lord in prayer, and His boundless mercy will shower you with endless love.

*****

Dear God,

Thank you for providing me the blessings of your Son dying on the cross for my sins. Be with me and show me your grace so I may share your love with others. Amen.

MARCH 17

> A good man out of the good treasure of his heart bringeth-forth that which is good; and an evil man out of the evil treasure of his heart bringth forth that which is evil: for of the abundance of the heart his mouth speaketh. (Luke 6:45)

Watch your words. Your mind may not be thinking clearly, and words may come out of your mouth that are not kind. Your emotions may overcome a fear that is bothering you at the time.

Take a step back and reflect what God would want you to say in that particular situation. Take out your Bible and turn to one of your favorite passages. Try to find comfort in knowing that God does hear your every thought and action.

Share your passage with a family member. Talk about a positive comment that you take away from the topic. It may be the best thought you had for that day.

*****

Dear God,

Thank you for listening to my words that I speak. Guide me through my thoughts and actions so I can witness to others. Amen.

MARCH 18

> What time I am afraid, I will trust in thee.
> (Psalm 56:3)

Everyone has a fear in life. Overcoming that fear or facing the unknown may be an uphill battle. When you are afraid, remember God is by your side and will guide you through the struggles you are facing.

God wants you to put your trust in Him. Take your fear and look at it from a different perspective. If you are afraid of the dark, use a flashlight to guide you through a room. If you fear being around a big crowd, only go to small group events and find someone to talk to during the event. There may be other people at the event who feel the same way you feel. Take life slowly, and you will soon develop your own energy level you feel comfortable with.

*****

Dear God,

Thank you for being with me when I am afraid. Please send your guardian angel to watch over me when fear comes to me again. Amen.

MARCH 19

> I do set my bow in the cloud, and it shall be for a token of a covenant between me and the earth. (Genesis 9:13)

Rainbows are beautiful. The many colors it displays. God's handiwork when He created the rainbow is such a reminder of His love for you. When you see a rainbow, it represents God's promise to you. He loves you.

The next time you see a rainbow, try to set a goal to create something positive in your life. It could be as simple as walking every day or calling a friend once a week to catch up on old times.

It's the act of putting your mind to something and then accomplishing that task. You are on your way to something great, so don't look back.

*****

Dear God,

Thank you for showing me your rainbow of life. Be with me to share your rainbow with others. Amen.

MARCH 20

> Therefore I say unto you, Take no thought for your life, what ye shall eat, or what ye shall drink; nor yet for your body, what ye shall put on. Is not the life more than meat, and the body than raiment?. (Matthew 6:25)

Do you ever question yourself about life? Do you have enough food to eat this week? God does not want you to worry about food, but instead concentrate on living life.

Some questions to think about:

- What was the best part of your day?
- What was the worst part of your day?
- Did you learn a lesson from today?
- What can you do to have a better day tomorrow?

These are some ideas to consider, knowing God knows all your thoughts and actions. Use the favorite saying, "What would Jesus do?" WWJD is familiar with a lot of Christians.

*****

Dear God,

Thank you for looking after me and taking care of my life. I may not always do the right thing but guide me to follow your example to witness to others. Amen.

MARCH 21

> A man's heart deviseth his way: but the
> Lord directeth his steps. (Proverbs 16:9)

God made plans for you before you were even born. He knew your identity and created you in His likeness. He loved you so much and had specific things in mind for you to do in the future.

Fast forward to reality, do you think you have accomplished what God had planned for you? You probably have sinned along the way, but God doesn't look at your faults; He only sees the good in you.

It is important to make good decisions in life, so they are pleasing to God. God does look down and can tell what you are thinking and doing. That's why God is a loving God, and he wants you to show that same love to others. As you go through life, try to witness daily to others, even if it is a simple gesture as, "Have a nice day."

*****

Dear God,

Thank you for making plans for me. Guide me as I walk through life and share your love with others. Amen.

MARCH 22

> My sheep hear my voice, and I know them, and they follow me: And I give unto them eternal life; and they shall never perish, neither shall any man pluck them out of my hand. (John 10:27–28)

A shepherd is one who guides, protects, and watches over the flock. As sheep, you need God to watch over and protect you. You may wander through life and sometimes get lost.

You may make a bad decision in life, and then have to deal with the consequences. Don't dwell on the fault; turn to God in prayer and ask for forgiveness.

He is always there to hear your wants and needs. He offers you eternal life and salvation for your sins.

*****

Dear God,

Thank you for being my Shepherd when I needed you most. Be with me to share your love with others. Amen.

MARCH 23

He giveth power to the faint; and to them that have no might he increaseth strength. (Isaiah 40:29)

Where do you get your strength from? Some people focus on their way of living or the food they eat. Some people read the Bible daily to get nourishment from passages they read. Do you have a favorite way you get your strength?

God has created each person differently; no two people are alike. One person may be strong, and the other person may be a lightweight. God doesn't compare His children. All are the same in His eyes.

God looks at the inside of his children and builds them up spiritually. God loves you just the way you are. God wants you to stay focused on His Word and share His love with others.

*****

Dear God,

Thank you for giving me the strength when I am weary. Be with me to share Your Word with others I meet in your kingdom. Amen.

MARCH 24

> And therefore will the Lord wait, that he may be gracious unto you, and therefore will he be exalted, that he may have mercy upon you: for the Lord is a God of judgment: blessed are all they that wait for him. (Isaiah 30:18)

Christians have a hard time with waiting. Minutes seem like hours and hours seem like days. God may not always give you what you want; it may be what He thinks you need instead.

God blesses you and in return requests you to be patient. God is also patient with you. One example is waiting for Christmas to arrive. The thrill of surprise that builds up to that day seems like forever.

As the Christmas season arrives, take time and enjoy the season instead of rushing around buying presents or making the cookies. Try to slow down and listen to some Christmas music, pay close attention to the words of the song. You will get more perspective from the meaning of the song, than sometimes just singing the words.

*****

Dear God,

Thank you for sending Jesus to die on the cross for me to take away my sin. Be with me as I go out and tell others of your love. Amen

MARCH 25

> Know ye not that they which run in a race
> run all, but one receiveth the prize? So run, that
> ye may obtain. (1 Corinthians 9:24)

Do you know of someone who has run in a race? They usually wear lightweight clothing, not heavy clothing to weigh them down.

As you think of your life, you may be weighed down with burdens of life or have circumstances which may prevent you from running the race of life. Your job may be stressful and not permit you a lot of free time. You may be involved in quite a few community activities, preventing you from having time with your family. God wants you to choose your time carefully. Slow down and enjoy life.

In the summer, sit outside and listen to the birds sing; they don't seem to have a care in the world. They are enjoying life.

*****

Dear God,

Thank you for being with me during my race with life. Strengthen me to continue the race of life until I reach my last day and see you in heaven. Amen

MARCH 26

> And he said unto them, Come ye yourselves apart into a desert place, and rest a while: for there were many coming and going, and they had no leisure so much as to eat. (Mark 6:31)

Yes, rest is important. Rest from a hard day's work. Work can consist of different types of labor: a construction worker, a teacher, a gardener, or a student.

Whatever your work entails, at the end of the day, you need to rest. The work can be physical or mental. If the work is physical, then your bones or muscles will be tired. If the work is mental, then you may have a headache or be unable to focus on at the end of the day.

Either way, take the time to rest, clear your mind from obstacles in your way, and meditate or ask God to give you some comfort from your labor. Take your concern to God in prayer asking Him to make your faith strong in His Word.

*****

Dear God,

Thank you for providing me rest when I need it the most. Guide me to seek your assistance the next time I am faced with a tough day. Amen.

MARCH 27

> Let us draw near with a true heart in full assurance of faith, having our hearts sprinkled from an evil conscience, and our bodies washed with pure water. (Hebrews 10:22)

You should be proud of who you are. God has created you to be unique; not like anyone else in this world. Look how far you have come in life, from childhood to adulthood. As you look back at all those childhood memories, the people you have been with and the things you have done, what a world of blessings God has bestowed upon you.

God's creation is marvelous and to be part of it is very special. The next time you feel sad or alone, remember God is always by your side; you are never alone. Relish your personal growth and the many blessings you have received throughout your life.

Everyone learns from their mistakes. Knowing what you did wrong and correcting it, so it doesn't happen again is an important part of your journey.

*****

Dear God,

Thank you for being present in my life. Be with me as I go out and share Your Word with others in Your kingdom. Amen.

MARCH 28

> Create in me a clean heart, O God; and
> renew a right spirit within me. (Psalm 51:10)

Trust in yourself that you are capable of doing good for others. Practice serving others; it's a great feeling. You forget about any misfortunes that you may have. Being sensitive about your personal feelings is only natural, but if you look beyond yourself and want to help others, life can turn itself around.

Volunteering is a natural direction a lot of retirees will take when their working career has ended. The businesses that use volunteers are so grateful for their experience and knowledge. It's the best of both worlds when you volunteer.

God wants you to use your steadfast spirit to go out into the world and share His love with others.

*****

Dear God,

Thank you for creating me a clean heart. Keep me steadfast in your faith so I may walk in your path to heaven. Amen.

MARCH 29

> Therefore all things whatsoever ye would that men should do to you, do ye even so to them: for this is the law and the prophets. (Matthew 7:12)

The Golden Rule is a great verse. Treating others how you would like to be treated. Making those around you feel good about themselves and feel happy. Employers who treat their employees fairly will be able to retain their employees for a long time.

People like to feel respected and encouraged. It lifts a person up when you praise them. God wants you to be considerate of others even if you disagree with their thoughts.

The next time you are in a difficult situation, think twice before speaking and try to respond on a positive note. Be an encourager.

*****

Dear God,

Thank you for giving me the courage to see things your way. Help me to encourage others to follow your path to righteousness. Amen.

MARCH 30

> To them who by patient continuance in well
> doing seek for glory and honor and immortality,
> eternal life. (Romans 2:7)

Eternal life is a gift of Christ to believers. Jesus is referring to "if you did it unto others, then you did it unto me." If you helped a stranger, in God's eyes, you did it unto him.

Eternal life is the reward for being righteous with God. For the unrighteous person, God refers to them as going to everlasting punishment.

God does not want to separate you from the love of God. That love is from Christ Jesus our Lord.

What a wonderful feeling knowing you are a child of God and clothed in his righteousness.

Thanks be to God; He will provide you with eternal life for believing in him. God's blessings.

*****

Dear God,

Thank you for believing in me and giving me eternal life. You alone are the master of the universe. Be with me and protect me until my life here on earth is ended and I can join you in heaven. Amen.

MARCH 31

> As far as the east is from the west, so far
> hath he removed our transgressions from us.
> (Psalm 103:12)

God wants you to have has faith in Him so you are never alone. He hears your prayers and your struggles. Everything has a purpose, and you may not understand it now, but it will make sense later.

You may mess up in life, but God is there to comfort you. Seek his salvation by reading the Bible. The Bible can give you knowledge and stories of peace.

God forgives you your sins. Go and show kindness to others and forget about your own struggles. Take one day at a time. Keep the faith. There may be rough times in your journey through life. Take one step at a time and ask God for love and peace along the way.

*****

Dear God,

Thank you for having faith in me. Be with me on my journey through life and give me love and peace until I reach my heavenly home. Amen.

APRIL 1

> Grace be to you and peace from God the Father, and from our Lord Jesus Christ. (Galatians 1:3)

This is sometimes the text heard before sermons. This is a beautiful passage. It speaks about God's grace for you and every Christian.

His grace is a gift for you to make life more meaningful. To know someone loves you with such a passion is a tremendous gift from God.

The next time you hear that passage in church, consider all the blessings and peace God has bestowed upon you: your health, your family, and your lifestyle.

God's abundant grace is everywhere. From the sun in the morning to the moon in the evening. From the stars in the sky and their radiant formations to the rainbow visible after a rain—God's creation is abundant. Take time to enjoy his creation.

*****

Dear God,

Thank you for your creation. Be with me as I proclaim your handiwork to others in this world. Amen.

APRIL 2

> He hath shewed thee, O man, what is good;
> and what doth the Lord require of thee, but to
> do justly, and to love mercy, and to walk humbly
> with thy God? (Micah 6:8)

We like to dream about the future. Do you ever wonder where you will be in five years or ten years? Your life could take a new direction—family, friends, or lifestyle.

Challenge yourself. Try something new and exciting. Explore the world. Step outside your comfort zone.

God encourages you to do justly and show mercy to others. Walk the path of God as a humble servant.

The last part of this passage talks about Christ's comfort to you. He doesn't want your heart to be troubled; just lean on him for safety and security.

*****

Dear God,

Thank you for showing me your mercy and compassion. Guide me in the right direction as you would want me to go. Amen.

APRIL 3

> Put on the whole armor of God, that ye may be able to stand against the wiles of the devil.
> (Ephesians 6:11)

Wearing the spiritual armor of God provides you energy to resist the devil. The devil is constantly tempting you and tries to make bad things happen to you. God wants you to resist temptations from the devil. The devil may tempt you to say bad things or do bad things.

God does know what is happening since he is all-knowing. When you are upset, step back and think about what is wrong with the task you are doing and ask God to guide you in the right way to respond to the action.

Instead of overreacting to an unstable action, try to respond in a positive way. For example, if an appliance broke in your house, you try to fix the appliance on your own if the task is a small one; if it is considered a major repair, then you contact a local appliance dealer for assistance. No need to get upset; there are skilled people who can assist you with repairs.

*****

Dear God,

Thank you for providing me with your armor to protect me from harm and danger. Be with me in the future to provide peace when troubles come upon me. Amen.

APRIL 4

> Thy hands have made me and fashioned me: give me understanding, that I may learn thy commandments. (Psalm 119:73)

God's creation is spectacular. His workmanship shows you the wondrous works of his hands. From creating the world, the humans in the world, and everything in the world, God knew exactly what he wanted when he created the world.

God knows your strengths and weaknesses. He does ask that you obey his commandments. You may need to learn understanding to follow his commandments.

The church is a good place to start to understand how to follow his commands. The pastor's sermon each Sunday provides insight on how to live a godly life.

Listen closely to the next sermon your pastor preaches. Does it give you inspiration to improve your life or go out into the world and share God's Word with others? Take heed of the gospel the pastor shares with people; he is God's representative to share the good news with you. Be open to the instructions he provides you and be receptive how you can apply the message to your daily life.

*****

Dear God,

Thank you for giving me the understanding to follow your commandments. Guide me to share Your Word with others in this world. Amen.

APRIL 5

> Rejoice evermore. Pray without ceasing. In everything give thanks: for this is the will of God in Christ Jesus concerning you. (1 Thessalonians 5:16–18)

Give thanks to God for the many blessings he bestows upon you. Losing a friend or losing a pet is sometimes difficult to bear. God knows your heart hurts from a loss of someone close. He is always there and will hear your prayer.

Rejoicing always, even during the bad times, is what God asks of you. He wants your prayer requests to be constant in good and bad circumstances.

Thank God during hard times and know he will guide you through every trial you experience, even if it is your worst day. Prayer does work. Pray to God when you feel alone and then wait for his response.

*****

Dear God,

Thank you for the many blessings you have bestowed upon me throughout my life. Protect me and guide me as life's struggles can be challenging at times. Amen.

APRIL 6

> He that loveth pureness of heart, for the grace of his lips the king shall be his friend. (Proverbs 22:11)

The way you live your life is between you and God. Having a pure heart means your motives are God pleasing, and you don't need to worry about what others think because you are honoring God.

Friends and family will be attracted to you so they can become just like you. God is always watching you. Your friends and family probably have the same interests as you do.

God doesn't want you to be a people pleaser but instead a Jesus pleaser; always looking for ways to do good in Jesus's sight.

Take your prayer requests to God and ask him to make you pure and holy in his sight.

*****

Dear God,

Thank you for giving me a pure heart. Be with me and give me your everlasting salvation so I can share your love with others. Amen.

APRIL 7

> Hearken unto this, O Job: stand still, and
> consider the wondrous works of God. (Job 37:14)

Be still or silent and listen to what God is trying to tell you. God wants to share His Word with you. He is commanding you to stand still so he can reason with you and show forth the righteous acts of the Lord, which he did for you and people before you.

Being still may be difficult for some people. People are constantly moving and doing activities in their life. If you stop and meditate in God's Word, what a quiet peace of mind you will experience.

Try focusing on meditation first thing in the morning before your busy day gets started; you only need five minutes. It could be that time when you are in the shower in the morning. Or maybe the last five minutes before you close your eyes at night.

*****

Dear God,

Thank you for having me be silent in Your Word. Guide me to focus on meditation in Your Word on my prayer journey. Amen.

APRIL 8

> Wherefore seeing we also are compassed about with so great a cloud of witnesses, let us lay aside every weight, and the sin which doth so easily beset us, and let us run with patience the race that is set before us, Looking unto Jesus the author and finisher of our faith; who for the joy that was set before him endured the cross, despising the shame, and is set down at the right hand of the throne of God. (Hebrews 12:1–2)

Maybe you have a competition or event you are in. You are asked to run with all you've got. Give it your all. Yes, God also wants you to "give it your all" in life. Be the best you can be. Focus on the task at hand or the completed project to reach the finish line.

Just when you want to give up, the adrenaline kicks in and you get the gusto to charge forward. If you think of God as your coach, the feeling of victory is right around the corner.

So your next challenge you are faced with in life, keep your focus on Jesus to finish your race strong to the end.

*****

Dear God,

Thank you for your perseverance in my race for life. Guide me and protect me when I face my next challenge in life. Keep me strong in Your Word. Amen.

APRIL 9

> For thou hast possessed my reins: thou hast
> covered me in my mother's womb. (Psalm 139:13)

God created you unique and can identify your specific traits. He knows your likes and dislikes along with your thoughts and actions.

Your family and friends may say they know your habits, but only God knows your intimate characteristics. That's why you trust God with your concerns through your prayers. Taking your cares and wants to him gives you the satisfaction that someone is listening to you.

If you ever get separated from God, in a trying period of your life, take time to search the Bible to get grounded in His Word. The Bible has all the answers you will ever need.

*****

Dear God,

Thank you for creating me in your likeness. Be with me and guide me to share Your Word with others in this world. Amen.

APRIL 10

> And he that searcheth the hearts knoweth what is the mind of the Spirit, because he maketh intercession for the saints according to the will of God. (Romans 8:27)

God knows your hidden talents. Everyone has skills; some may be apparent, and some may be yet to be unearthed. You may be a leader in your church or community or may be a worker. Workers gain experience the more they do the task; eventually that person may take on a leader role in the future.

You may take a photography class and then end of taking photos and framing them and selling at a local event. The opportunities are endless.

Another example may be attending a weekend retreat and meeting new people who have some of the same interests that you do. You are glad you took that opportunity to try that adventure.

God gave you the covenant. Be prepared to witness for God each day. There are many who have not heard the gospel. Share it with others; you'll be glad you did.

*****

Dear God,

Thank you for showing me my hidden talents. You alone know my thoughts and actions. Guide me in the future to venture out and find my new talents. Amen.

APRIL 11

> Praying always with all prayer and supplication in the Spirit and watching thereunto with all perseverance and supplication for all saints. (Ephesians 6:18)

Prayer is a powerful tool. Prayer gets you through some difficult situations in life. God hears your prayers and supplications and will respond in the best way possible. Trust in God and it shall come to pass. God is all-knowing and all-powerful. The Bible provides instruction on how to live your daily life.

Thank God every day for the many blessings he bestows upon you. Your health, your family, and your church are just a few of the blessings you have in your life that make you a better person.

Start your prayer life today; you will be amazed at the difference it will make in your life.

*****

Dear God,

Thank you for sending Jesus into my life. Embrace me to grow my prayer life to your satisfaction. You alone are my strength and provider. Amen.

APRIL 12

> Come unto me, all ye that labor and are heavy laden, and I will give you rest. (Matthew 11:28)

Have you had a burden you carried for some time, hoping it would get better? Maybe over time your situation resolved. But at the time, it seemed unrelenting and cumbersome.

Everyone has struggles in their life. Being patient and dealing with the situation is the real challenge. God in his mercy wants you to give him your struggles and let him resolve them for you. Researching the Bible is a good start. Taking your burdens to God in prayer is another answer.

God is there to give you rest from your heavy burden. There is no perfect person, but God is there to comfort you when life gets overwhelming. Take that first step to take it to God in prayer to get you through the rough times.

Open up your heart and experience the glory from above. God's abundant grace is for everyone on earth. Try sharing His love with others around you.

*****

Dear God,

Thank you for carrying my heavy burden when my life gets tough. Be with me to share your love with others I come in contact with. Amen.

APRIL 13

> But the Lord said unto Samuel, Look not on his countenance, or on the height of his stature; because I have re-fused him: for the Lord seeth not as man seeth; for man looketh on the outward appearance, but the Lord looketh on the heart. (1 Samuel 16:7)

Is true beauty your outward appearance? No, true beauty is your inward appearance, what God sees within you. Some physical traits make a person attractive or not attractive to the human eye.

Some people have been blessed with beauty. God does not look down on a person for their outward appearance.

God shows his love to all mankind; everyone is beautiful in God's eyes. God knows what is in your heart and how kind and compassionate you are to others.

By showing God's love to others, God is looking down on you and giving you a big smile. His love is contagious; pass it on!

*****

Dear God,

Thank you for creating me and looking at my inward appearance instead of my outward appearance. Be with me and protect me on my journey to my eternal home. Amen.

APRIL 14

> Blessed be God, even the Father of our Lord
> Jesus Christ, the Father of mercies, and the God
> of all comfort. (2 Corinthans 1:3)

When you are hurt or upset and there is no one to hear you, go to God in prayer. He is your comforter and will listen to your little details. Even if you have unkind thoughts, he is there to console you and understands what you are thinking.

Go to a quiet place and share your thoughts with God. Release your burdens, and as soon as you do, you will feel better that you were able to express your thoughts.

God is considered a secret keeper and listens to your every thought and action. You can go to God in prayer any time of day, and you know he is there for you.

Start each day with Jesus in prayer and soon it will come to be a good habit to have. Also, ending each day with prayer is just as beneficial for your prayer life.

*****

Dear God,

Thank you for sending Jesus to take away my sins. Be with me as I begin my prayer life every day with you. Amen.

APRIL 15

> Let all bitterness, and wrath, and anger, and clamor, and evil speaking, be put away from you, with all malice: And be ye kind one to another, tenderhearted, forgiving one another, even as God for Christ's sake hath forgiven you. (Ephesians 4:31–32)

Have you ever experienced bitterness or anger toward another person? At the time, you think you are right. But in God's eyes, it is not the right decision. God warns you to rid yourself of bitterness and anger or any evil behavior. Show kindness to one another, forgiving as he forgave you.

Try to have a soft heart to the person who you may have had harsh words with. Turn the other cheek and demonstrate compassion or empathy toward them.

God is counting you to share your faith as a Christian-like person. A little kindness can go a long way.

*****

Dear God,

Thank you for helping me get rid of bitterness in my life. Be with me to show more kindness to those around me. Amen.

APRIL 16

> Blessed are they that do his commandments, that they may have right to the tree of life and may enter in through the gates into the city. (Revelation 2:14)

God wants you to read the Bible, but also to live bold in your life through his Word. Your actions speak louder than words. Embrace your life, take one day at a time, focus on meditation and how you can improve one aspect of your life today. Tomorrow is another day, but for some people, tomorrow may not come. Treat each day as a blessing from God.

God provides many blessings to us each day; it could be as simple as the morning sunshine to make us smile or a restful night's sleep to provide energy to get through the day.

God is your provider, and he is your ever-present help in need. Go to God with your requests and ask for his direction and guidance.

*****

Dear God,

Provide me with guidance to embrace my life and follow in your footsteps. You are truly my ever-present help in need. Amen.

APRIL 17

> Be not ye therefore like unto them: for your Father knoweth what things ye have need of, before ye ask him. (Matthew 6:8)

Waiting for a response from a prayer request may take time. Instead of an instant response, God may provide a delayed response or maybe "not at this time" response. God does hear your prayers, but not all the requests may be important concerns.

For example, if you are on a committee for a big event in your community where everyone has specific tasks to do, and then the event is cancelled due to weather, that's a perfect example of what God is showing you that he knows all things. Maybe the event was a fundraiser for the community and a lot of time was put in to organizing and planning it. Sometimes unforeseen circumstances occur preventing the event to happen. Likewise, God does hear your supplications and provides a response when the time is right. Don't give up on God, because he will not give up on you.

*****

Dear God,

Thank you for being the all-knowing God. Be with me and protect me as I minister to others in Your kingdom. Amen.

APRIL 18

> And seek not ye what ye shall eat, or what ye shall drink, neither be ye of doubtful mind.
> (Luke 12:29)

Do you have stress in your life? Everyone has some kind of stress. How you deal with the stress is what counts.

God asks you to pray about your stress. Tell God what you need and thank him for what he has done in your life. God has been by your side through all your ups and downs. He has always been there for you. God grants you his peace and understanding.

God's peace is like the calming of the sea. It brings reassurance that life will get better if you look to God for guidance.

Try to keep your stress level low and continue to pray to God for guidance in your life.

The next time you need some strength in your life, go to God in prayer and ask for some strength to get you through that difficult situation. He will give you the confidence you need to tackle the task at hand.

*****

Dear God,

Thank you for being with me during stressful times in my life. Help me focus on Your scripture for guidance during life's difficult days. Amen.

APRIL 19

> Put on therefore, as the elect of God, holy and beloved, bowels of mercies, kindness, humbleness of mind, meekness, longsuffering; Forbearing one another, and forgiving one another, if any man have a quarrel against any: even as Christ forgave you, so also do ye. (Colossians 3:12–13)

As children of God, you are special in God's eyes. God chose you to be his own. God has clothed you with compassion, kindness, and patience. He wants your happiness to be priority today.

Take control of your joy and spread your joy to those around you. Be in the moment. Focus every living moment on Christ and the many blessings he has bestowed upon you. Every day thank God for your health, your home to live in, your job to provide for your family, and your faith to keep you going every day.

By choosing you, God has great expectations of you. Go out into the world and show his love to others. Express yourself to others by sharing that act of kindness with those around you.

*****

Dear God,

Thank you for having me part of your chosen people. Be with me as I go out into the world and show love to others as you would want me to do. Amen.

APRIL 20

> But lay up for yourselves treasures in heaven, where neither moth nor rust doth corrupt, and where thieves do not break through nor steal. (Matthew 6:20)

What are your treasures you are taking with you to heaven? Many people are looking forward to seeing their loved ones someday in heaven. Others are looking forward to seeing Jesus. While others may be looking forward to a pain-free environment if they have had chronic pain in their life.

To God be the glory, you should look forward to heaven and its marvelous beauty. God has promised you eternal life, and it will be worth the wait.

Have you prepared yourself for heaven? Ask an elderly person and they may answer that you read the Bible, sing songs relating to their heavenly home, or may talk about their loved ones who have gone to heaven before them. Please think about how you will prepare yourself for heaven.

*****

Dear God,

Thank you for giving me eternal life. Be with me as I prepare for heaven and someday see you on your royal throne. Amen.

APRIL 21

> The merciful man doeth good to his own
> soul: but he that is cruel troubleth his own flesh.
> (Proverbs 11:17)

Showing kindness to others may sound easier than it really is. Going out of your way to do a nice gesture for someone is a good example. If the person thanks you for the gesture, that makes you feel good inside. What if the person shows no acknowledgement for the kind act you showed them and maybe just ignored that act. Wow! Makes you stop and think twice if you would do that kind gesture again.

God does know what you do and your thoughts. He is aware of your actions. Please continue your kind and compassionate heart as he believes in you.

Cruelty and evil will get you nowhere. Eternal life is yours, just keep focused on His Word.

*****

Dear God,

Thank you for showing me your kindness and mercy by ending Jesus to take away my sins. Be with me to show others kindness throughout the world. Amen.

APRIL 22

> That I may publish with the voice of thanksgiving and tell of all thy wondrous works. (Psalm 26:7)

Have you ever had a close call when driving and barely missed having an accident? Maybe you were distracted and not paying attention to the road. Sometimes in life you encounter close calls and God is protecting you from harm and danger.

Do you ever thank God for protecting you from the danger? Thanks be to God for his great works. He is always there for you when you are in harm's way.

You should be thanking God every day for giving you life and for giving you another day to share his love with others around you. Praise be to God for your health and for being on this earth another day.

God will tell you when the timing is right. Take his lead and venture out. You can be one of God's disciples, even if it is only in a small way.

*****

Dear God,

Thank you for giving me another day on this earth. Be with me to spread your gospel to others in this world. Amen.

APRIL 23

> But his delight is in the law of the Lord;
> and in his law doth he meditate day and night.
> (Psalm 1:2)

You are privileged to be in a country to be able to share the Word of God with others. Some countries are restrictive on what its citizens can read.

God wants you to read and share His gospel with others. You should have a thirst for living a life full of faith and hope in Jesus.

When a new pastor shares his first sermon with a new congregation, he is so full of life and enthusiasm; it is very contagious. His congregation welcomes his inspiring words to live by.

God inspires him and provides the voice to share God's Word with others.

Thank your pastor the next time you see him and tell him how much you appreciate his sermons and the messages he shares to the congregation.

*****

Dear God,

Thank you for providing the Bible to me and others in this world. Be with me and guide me as I share Your Word with others. Amen.

APRIL 24

> Jesus saith unto him, I am the way, the truth, and the life: no man cometh unto the Father, but by me. (John 14:6)

The passage refers to Christ as truth and grace. It can also be said that Christ is the life. He is the mediator between people and God and eternal life.

Christ being the life refers to radiant life, abundant life, and also life everlasting. Since you believe in God so you should be filled with righteousness.

Are you filled with God's truth and grace? Do you need to be enriched with God's wisdom? Look around you and explore opportunities where you could volunteer or help individuals with daily activities in life. You will be amazed at how much church or community involvement there is available.

The rewards are great when you give of yourself to improve life for others.

*****

Dear God,

Thank you for showering me with your truth and grace. Guide me on my journey to share your life with others. Amen.

APRIL 25

> Be of good courage, and he shall strengthen your heart, all ye that hope in the Lord. (Psalm 31:24)

What are you afraid of? Could it be volunteering at an event and maybe asked to speak in public? Or maybe you are asked to collect money for an event and feel uncomfortable asking for money from people. Whatever your fear, God hears your thoughts. God will give you the courage and comfort to face your fears.

The next time you are asked to help with an event or serve on a committee, simply say yes and then ask God in a silent prayer to give you the courage to serve him gladly.

*****

Dear God,

Thank you for keeping me strong and giving me the courage to serve you. Grant me peace to tackle new opportunities I am presented with and to share your love with others. Amen.

APRIL 26

> Thou art my hiding place; thou shalt preserve me from trouble; thou shalt compass me about with songs of deliverance. Selah. (Psalm 32:7)

Do you have a favorite hiding place you go to when you are scared? God knows your thoughts and actions and will protect you from harm.

Life can be scary at times. When you feel uncomfortable at work, with friends, or at home, take a step back and analyze how God would handle the situation. Prayer works wonders. Say a prayer to God for protection. God will put his loving arms around you and comfort you during those scary times.

So the next time you feel scared, think of a favorite Bible passage and repeat it a couple of times. God is with you and will be your hiding place.

*****

Dear God,

Thank you for being my hiding place when I am scared. Be with me when I am faced with uncertainty in life and protect me. Amen.

APRIL 27

> Finally, my brethren, be strong in the Lord, and in the pow-er of his might. Put on the whole armor of God, that ye may be able to stand against the wiles of the devil. (Ephesians 6:10–11)

These passages refer to being a soldier. Being strong in the Lord, powered by his might and putting on the armor of God is his faith in you. He wants you to stand up to the devil and not get tempted.

God is your strength and encourages you to be strong and resist the devil and his destructive ways.

Are you a soldier in God's army? Are you strong in your faith? Can you resist temptations if they want you to do wrong?

You can start today to be strong. Open your heart and let Jesus in. He is your stronghold and can guide you down the path of righteousness. Let Jesus in your life today.

*****

Dear God,

Thank you for being the stronghold of my life. Be with me and guide me to share your love with others. Amen.

APRIL 28

> When he gave to the sea his decree, that the waters should not pass his commandment: when he appointed the foundations of the earth. (Proverbs 8:29)

God gave the waters a boundary or shoreline. He wanted to hold back the water to save the land for his people. In life, people also have boundaries or rules to follow. When you attend a sports event, only the athletes are allowed on the playing field. The spectators stand behind the fence for safety.

Rules are made to be obeyed. If the rules are not followed, harm could occur if going outside the boundaries. Staying within the boundaries is tempting, and you may feel you are missing out on the fun. An example is, when you are at the sporting event and want to get a signature from one of the popular players on the field, you may want to do whatever is possible to get that signature.

God wants you to stop and rethink your decision. God knows best and encourages you to stay within your boundaries.

*****

Dear God,

Thank you for making boundaries in my life. Protect me from all harm and danger in my future endeavors. Amen.

APRIL 29

> And let the peace of God rule in your hearts,
> to the which also ye are called in one body; and
> be ye thankful. (Colossians 3:15)

By letting peace rule in your heart, God is directing you down the right path to follow. You may be tempted by others in your life to form bad habits; just turn away from the devil. Listen to God. God wants you to listen to your heart and do the right thing.

God is giving you the gift of peace of mind. Follow his lead to go down the right path.

The importance of this text is to listen. God gives you hints of ways to follow his example. One way is to read the Bible and find his love throughout scripture. It's not enough to hear his word, but also to live your life by his example.

*****

Dear God,

Thank you for giving peace to my heart. I know it is a tough job to follow your lead. Guide me and direct me to a life pleasing to you. Amen.

APRIL 30

> But know that the Lord hath set apart him
> that is godly for himself: the Lord will hear when
> I call unto him. (Psalm 4:3)

Hearing is one of your senses that you use every day. You hear your phone ring and try to answer it right away. If someone is trying to reach you by phone, they may leave a message if you are not available. Or they may text you, which is very popular in today's world. Out of courtesy, you should respond to the message or text to find out what they wanted.

When you request something from God you also need to wait for an answer. The answer could come right away or maybe the timing is not right and God may delay responding to you.

This is when you learn patience. Patience is a godly thing. You shouldn't be in a hurry in life. Life happens very fast; taking time to enjoy life and have patience will help you enjoy life to the fullest.

*****

Dear God,

Thank you for listening to me when I make requests known to you in prayer. Teach me to be more patient in my daily life. Amen.

MAY 1

> Blessed are the poor in spirit: for theirs is
> the kingdom of heaven. (Matthew 5:3)

This passage relates to humility. As you read this passage, think about all the blessings you have received throughout your life. God has been good to you.

You can thank God for your health, your family, and your current lifestyle. God knows your thoughts and actions and has provided abundantly for your needs.

If you think back through the years, your life has really changed. Growing up, you listened to your parents and the life lessons they gave you. When you were in school, your teachers provided you with insight on what you would need to face the world. At work, your employer provides training to do an occupation.

Throughout life, there are lessons to be learned. Sit back and enjoy the ride and take in the valuable lessons God provides through various people you come in contact with. Life is good.

*****

Dear God,

Thank you for giving me humility. It keeps me grounded in your word. Be with me and protect me as I travel through life's adventures. Amen.

MAY 2

> Blessed are they that mourn: for they shall be comforted. (Matthew 5:4)

Trials and tribulations are a part of life. Everyone has them. God knows when life can be difficult for you. He is there to comfort you and get you through the tough times.

God has a new door of life for you. As you walk through the new door, dream what life will be like with God as your master; He will lead you on down paths you could never have imagined. You will meet new people in your life who will inspire you to be your best.

Your church family is always there for you to support you when life is challenging.

If the opportunity is available, take the time to volunteer. Volunteering could be in your community, your church, or helping a family member in need. Your inner spirit will come out and show you the strength you never knew you had before.

*****

Dear God,

Thank you for giving me trials and tribulations. It has made me stronger in Your Word. Guide me through life as I focus on sharing your love with others. Amen.

MAY 3

> Blessed are the meek: for they shall inherit the earth. (Matthew 5:5)

Are you satisfied with your life? Your wants and needs are different than they were five to ten years ago. As you go through life, what you wanted yesterday may be totally different than your needs are today.

God knows your wants and needs. He provides for you what he feels you need to fulfill your daily life. He wants you to dream big. Maybe even change your life for the better.

Try creating a vision board and placing pictures on it of places you would like to visit. You can always dream. Maybe just reading about the location at the local library is all you can do at the time. In the future, you may be able to actually visit one of your dream locations. Never give up. God doesn't give up on you.

*****

Dear God,

Thank you for keeping me meek in your spirit. Give me the strength to dream big in Your Word and go out into this world and share your love with others. Amen.

MAY 4

> Blessed are they which do hunger and thirst after righteousness: for they shall be filled. (Matthew 5:6)

Live a life of gratitude. God will fill your life with righteousness. God wants you to be fruitful and abounding in his love. As you embrace your gratitude, write down a list of some of your many blessings you have received over the years.

The abundance of love you have received from your family and friends has been gratifying. You may think you are lacking in gifts, but God provides for you what he thinks you need.

Reading the Bible, you will find many passages of God's love. He wants you to share his love with others. Be a cheerful giver. God is watching you.

*****

Dear God,

Thank you for making me take responsibility for my actions. Be with me to follow your path to eternal life. Amen.

MAY 5

> Blessed are the merciful: for they shall obtain mercy. (Matthew 5:7)

Are you merciful? Do you ask God to show mercy to you? This could be an emotional state of mind. Your intuition may be directing you one way and your emotions may be guiding you in a different direction.

Trust in God for the right way to go in life. Sometimes praying for guidance is beneficial. God knows your thoughts and actions. God's way may be different than your way.

Your lifestyle may be abundant in material things. Do you really need all those items? If you went a month without buying those material things, would you be happier?

Consider your wants and needs. Your life may change in a month's time if you consider making a lifestyle change.

*****

Dear God,

Thank you for showing mercy on me. Be with me and guide me as I make a lifestyle change in my life. Amen.

MAY 6

> Blessed are the pure in heart: for they shall see God. (Matthew 5:8)

Looking into the future may be scary, but if you are an adventurous person, it could be a new beginning in your life. Your future starts now. Taking that first step is always the hardest one.

The road may be less traveled, but you can be that person blazing the trail for others. You are never alone. God is always beside you. He wants you to create your own path in life.

Setting the standard can be exciting and others will look to you for your direction. Some ideas for your new path could be at church—starting a new group for members to get together, maybe once a month to socialize, or offering to start a new activity for school children after school or on the weekend.

The possibilities are endless. If you are not sure how to start your new adventure, talk to some of the people at your church or school who organize a lot of the events. They are always looking for new ideas to get church members involved. Remember God is your master.

*****

Dear God,

Thank you for making me pure at heart. Be with me to create a new path in my life to share your love in your kingdom. Amen.

MAY 7

> Blessed are the peacemakers: for they shall
> be called the children of God. (Matthew 5:9)

Forgiving. Do you always forgive? Sometimes it may be tough. God wants you to forgive and then move on. Resentments may be holding you back in life. When you forgive, you let go of the past and look to the future.

God is a forgiving God. He knows your mistakes and misfortunes and is always willing to wipe your slate clean. You are God's child, and he is your peacemaker. You have eternal life to look forward to in heaven, so let the past go and strive for a more positive future.

As you search scriptures, focus on praising and rejoicing God in his marvelous magnitude of blessings he has bestowed upon you. Your heart will be much lighter when you leave all your worries to God.

*****

Dear God,

Thank you for being my peacemaker. Grant me grace to always forgive and move on with my life. Amen.

MAY 8

> Blessed are they which are persecuted for righteousness' sake: for theirs is the kingdom of heaven. (Matthew 5:10)

Persecution—think of it as a spiritual awakening. You are waking up to new thoughts to process. Material things don't matter much anymore once you are spiritually enlightened. Your emotions take over, and God is with you to gain a more spiritual in-sight of what heaven is like.

You may go through bad days in your life, but God will be there for you. Trust in God for protection.

In the Bible, people were persecuted and harmed against their will. God was aware of the happenings. God wants you to have patience. Life can be trying at times. Trust in God that all will work out in the end. You have eternal life in heaven to look forward to. Give God the glory.

*****

Dear God,

Thank you for your righteousness and for sending Jesus to die on the cross for my sins. Be with me and grant me your peace. Amen.

MAY 9

> Blessed are ye, when men shall revile you, and persecute you, and shall say all manner of evil against you falsely, for my sake. (Matthew 5:11)

Have you ever been falsely accused of something? It doesn't make you feel good since you know the comment is not true. You need to stand strong and speak the truth. Eventually, the truth will set you free.

God knows the truth and is there to give you direction on how to handle the situation. Letting go of the issue is difficult, but forgiving is the right thing to do.

The person who falsely accused you may have had the devil on their side. Just envision the person you need to forgive and focus on the Godly reaction to resolve the situation.

God is all-knowing and will put words in your head to guide you to lighten your heart. You may need a day to think about your actions. Be confident. God is with you all the way.

*****

Dear God,

Thank you for being with me during the bad times in my life. Be with me to show others the love you gave me and to learn to forgive others. Amen.

MAY 10

> And they brought young children to him, that he should touch them: and his disciples rebuked those that brought them. But when Jesus saw it, he was much displeased, and said unto them, Suffer the little children to come unto me, and forbid them not: for of such is the kingdom of God. Verily I say unto you, whosoever shall not receive the kingdom of God as a little child, he shall not enter therein. And he took them up in his arms, put his hands upon them, and blessed them. (Mark 10:13–16)

Baptism belongs to everyone. What a beautiful passage of Christ blessing the little children.

It is special to witness a baptism in church. God is welcoming another child into his kingdom. Baptism can happen at any age. Adults do get baptized later in life. God has open arms when it comes to eternal life in heaven.

Think back to the last time you experienced a baptism of one of your family members. What a joyous occasion! And what an important role the sponsors or godparents play in bringing up the child in the admonition of the Lord.

Just remember, the next time you witness baptism, think of yourself and how special you are in God's eyes.

*****

Dear God,

Thank you for the sacrament of baptism. Be with me to share your love to all, including the newly baptized children. Amen.

MAY 11

> And Ruth said, Intreat me not to leave thee, or to return from following after thee: for whither thou goest, I will go; and where thou lodgest, I will lodge: thy people shall be my people, and thy God my God: where thou diest, will I die, and there will I be buried: the Lord do so to me, and more also, if ought but death part thee and me. (Ruth 1:16–17)

Friendship is a wonderful thing. Everyone needs friends. Even though the relationship in the scripture is mother-in-law and daughter-in-law, it is a very special connection between the two of them.

It was a wise choice to stay together. They were chosen for each other. God chose you to be his child. You are very special in his eyes.

God is asking you to make a wise choice and choose him and the Bible. He encourages you to read the Bible daily and then live your life accordingly. Life is too short, so choose wisely.

*****

Dear God,

Thank you for being my friend. Be with me as I share your love with others in Your kingdom. Amen.

MAY 12

> Lord, thou hast been our dwelling place in all generations. Before the mountains were brought forth, or ever thou hadst formed the earth and the world, even from everlasting to everlasting, thou art God. (Psalm 90:1–2)

Creation! What a beautiful thing God has made. If you ever have an opportunity, visit the national parks and marvel at God's beauty. Or take note of all the flowers when they are in full bloom in the summer around your community.

God truly is magnificent. Your eternal God is everywhere and does everything. He wants you to enjoy your time on this earth. He is your divine refuge in time of need and will provide you with what he thinks you need.

If you have a need, ask God in prayer for assistance. He is all-knowing and all-powerful. Give him the opportunity to satisfy your needs.

*****

Dear God,

Thank you for giving me eternal life. Guide me down the path of righteousness so I can be with you in heaven someday. Amen.

MAY 13

> It is a good thing to give thanks unto the Lord, and to sing praises unto thy name, O most High: To shew forth thy loving kindness in the morning, and thy faithfulness every night, Upon an instrument of ten strings, and upon the psaltery; upon the harp with a solemn sound. (Psalm 92:1–3)

Praise God with thanksgiving using your voice to sing songs to his glory. God shows his loving kindness to you through your friends and family. You may be blessed with an abundance of both.

Having family and friends around you when sharing momentous occasions or events is very special. It makes the event even more fun when there is someone there to share it with and laugh or celebrate together.

God does ask you to show your faithfulness to him through your actions with others. He encourages you to study the Bible with others at church and then discuss the importance of God's Word. The Bible should be your focus to start every day.

*****

Dear God,

Thank you for letting me praise you every day. Guide me to witness to others as you would want me to on this earth. Amen.

MAY 14

> Let your light so shine before men, that they
> may see your good works, and glorify your Father
> which is in heaven. (Matthew 5:16)

Glorify God and His good works. Your Father looks down on earth and knows your actions and thoughts. You worship Him and glorify His holy name every Sunday when you sing hymns of praise to Him.

Letting your light shine to others is what God wants you to do every day. He wants you to study the Bible and live what is preached to you on Sundays.

Your actions are noticed by others, so it is important to always put your best foot forward in sharing his love with others.

Small gestures on a daily basis could be smiling at strangers, calling a friend and asking how they are doing, or telling someone to have a good day. These are all small acts of kindness, and anyone can share the love with others every day.

*****

Dear God,

Thank you for shining your light upon me. Be with me so I can share your love among mankind. Amen.

MAY 15

> For every house is built by some man; but
> he that built all things is God. (Hebrews 3:4)

God is referring to the church when he compares it to a building. Just as it takes time to construct a building, so does God's work to make a small congregation into a large one. It is having constant conversation with the workers who are constructing the building. So as the congregation forms committees to try to attract new members to the church.

When the congregation has its building all constructed, they may have an open house to show the new building to the community. Likewise, a congregation may advertise to the community a meet and greet for prospective new members to take a tour of the church and learn a little more about the congregation and its rich history. Some of the favorite tours in a congregation include learning the significance of the church windows. Someone from your local congregation may even document the significance of each of the windows and its meaning in biblical time.

*****

Dear God,

Thank you for building my church for me to worship in. Keep me strong in your word so I may share your love with others. Amen.

MAY 16

> And these things write we unto you, that
> your joy may be full. (1 John 1:4)

John wrote this epistle to the believers to add joy to their hearts. What a beautiful passage to be so full of joy.

Joy is very popular at Christmastime. Many signs with the word *joy* either in their homes or outside as a Christmas decoration.

God wants you to have joy in your heart all year long. With the happenings in the world today, sadness exists in many hearts. Focusing on God's Word can bring joy to people who have heavy hearts and are hurting.

As one church refers to JOY as "just older youth," you can be any age to experience the joy of God and share his love to others. Go and spread some joy today.

*****

Dear God,

Thank you for giving me joy in my life. Be with me to share your love and joy with others in your kingdom. Amen.

MAY 17

> My little children, these things write I unto you, that ye sin not. And if any man sin, we have an advocate with the Father, Jesus Christ the righteous: And he is the propitiation for our sins: and not for ours only, but also for the sins of the whole world. (1 John 2:1–2)

Little children are referred to as believers. God wants you to have the mind of a little child. To believe that his word is true. He wants to be the mediator for you against sin and the devil.

God is your protector and knows your thoughts and actions.

When you are faced with a difficult situation, ask God to protect you. He is there to support you in your adversity. God is love. God's love is always there when life gets tough. Take comfort in knowing there is a God who loves you dearly.

*****

Dear God,

Thank you for believing in me and guarding me from sin and the devil. Protect me from all harm and danger so I can share your love with others. Amen.

MAY 18

> And now abideth faith, hope, charity, these three; but the greatest of these is charity. (1 Corinthians 13:13)

The passage talks about the three graces: faith, hope, and charity with charity as the greatest of the graces. The verse can also be referred to as "the enduring" or those things that abide. The "seen" things are called temporal, while the unseen things are referred to as eternal. So true is God's Word. We read the Bible and try to understand its meaning even though it may be unseen.

As you focus on faith, hope, and charity, try to imagine the spiritual love God gives every day in your life. Look around you and feel the love from your family to your neighbors. Why not reciprocate the gesture and invite a friend to go to an event with you. The outing may be just what the friend needs to do outside of their comfort zone.

*****

Dear God,

Thank you for shining down on me with your faith, hope, and charity. Grant me wisdom to know and do your will. Amen.

MAY 19

> These things have I written unto you that believe on the name of the Son of God; that ye may know that ye have eternal life, and that ye may believe on the name of the Son of God. (1 John 5:13)

The passage talks about strength and faith in Christ. All believers are assured eternal life with Christ.

God wants you to have the spiritual knowledge of knowing you are going to heaven when your earthly life is done. What an inspiring thought to know believers have their faith redeemed in the love of God.

When attending a funeral, many people talk about their loved one and the memories they shared.

You may be sad to lose them, but God has other plans for them in heaven. You should be glad for them as they are going to their eternal home. And you will be joining them someday. So rejoice in the Lord.

*****

Dear God,

Thank you for strengthening my faith in you. Be with me to share your love with others. Amen.

MAY 20

> Beloved, I wish above all things that thou mayest prosper and be in health, even as thy soul prospereth. (3 John 1:2)

Good health. Everyone wants it. If you have good health, studies show you will live longer. Eating the right foods and exercise may also contribute to a healthier long life.

God also emphasizes spiritual growth. Reading and studying the Bible promotes a healthy life in His Word. God wants you to share his love with others. Even the simple acts of kindness are showing his love. Smiling at someone or asking how someone is doing is showing love or acting that you care about their well-being.

Make it a daily activity to show love to just one person a day. And soon it may be two or three people a day that you will be sharing acts of kindness with.

*****

Dear God,

Thank you for giving me my health. Strengthen me to show your love to others. Amen.

MAY 21

> For I rejoiced greatly, when the brethren came and testified of the truth that is in thee, even as thou walkest in the truth. I have no greater joy than to hear that my children walk in truth. (3 John 1:3–4)

Are you a consistent Christian, walking in the truth? Do you experience spiritual joy in your daily life? If you answered yes to these questions, then your walk with Jesus is fulfilling. You should be walking in truth and feeling joyful every day on this earth.

God put you on this earth to enjoy life to the fullest. If you are not enjoying life, then look around and find something that makes you joyful. Love and joy are all around you. You just need to tap into that emotion to find it.

Meeting people may be a start to find love or joy. Volunteer at a church or community event. There are always a lot of people you can meet and share ideas with. If you enjoy the company of others, then volunteer more days of the week if your schedule allows it. The important thing is to get started. God bless you in your new adventure.

*****

Dear God,

Thank you for walking with me in my walk of truth. Be with me and guide me to share your love with mankind. Amen.

MAY 22

> Beloved, thou doest faithfully whatsoever thou doest to the brethren, and to strangers; which have borne witness of thy charity before the church: whom if thou bring forward on their journey after a godly sort, thou shalt do well. (3 John 1:5–6)

Brotherly love is what God wants you to show to others every day. Having spiritual love and showing it to those around you is the godly thing to do. Are you helpful to strangers? What if you are walking down a sidewalk and a stranger stops and asks you for directions? Yes, you would be helpful and guide them on their way.

God looks at you with favor. It's a good feeling for you when you do a good deed for others.

God wants you to show hospitality to others when the need arises. If you were on vacation in a strange place and asked a stranger for assistance, wouldn't you be grateful for their kindness? Yes, you were put on this earth to show love to one another, just as God loves you.

*****

Dear God,

Thank you for showing brotherly love to me. Guide me to share your love with those around me on this earth. Amen.

MAY 23

> And beside this, giving all diligence, add to your faith virtue; and to virtue knowledge; And to knowledge temperance; and to temperance patience; and to patience godliness; And to godliness brotherly kindness; and to brotherly kindness charity. For if these things be in you, and abound, they make you that ye shall neither be barren nor unfruitful in the knowledge of our Lord Jesus Christ. (2 Peter 1:5–8)

These are the seven essential steps in your development of a spiritual life and fruitfulness.

1. Virtue: Your strong faith.
2. Knowledge: Knowing Jesus as your Savior.
3. Temperance: Keeping your temper intact.
4. Patience: Holding back your tongue and only speaking good thoughts.
5. Godliness: Giving thanks for all mankind.
6. Brotherly kindness: Showing affection to others around you.
7. Charity: The bond of perfection.

*****

Dear God,

Thank you for providing steps for spiritual living. Guide me on my journey to eternal life and protect me along the way. Amen.

MAY 24

> But the day of the Lord will come as a thief in the night; in the which the heavens shall pass away with a great noise, and the elements shall melt with fervent heat, the earth also and the works that are therein shall be burned up. Seeing then that all these things shall be dissolved, what manner of persons ought ye to be in all holy conversation and godliness. (2 Peter 3:10–11)

Judgement day…are you ready for it? God speaks about the last things you will do on this earth when the end draws near.

God wants you to be ready when the last day approaches. Just as people prepare their wills or last wishes with an attorney, so you should consider your last wishes in your life.

Have you told your family your last wishes when your end of life comes near?

It's something to consider. Talk to your pastor and family members and start making your wishes be known. You never know when God will call you to your eternal home.

*****

Dear God,

Thank you for asking me to prepare for my last day on this earth. My faith may be weak, but my trust is in you for guidance. Be with me in my daily life. Amen.

MAY 25

> Casting all your care upon him; for he careth for you. (1 Peter 5:7)

Do you get so busy with your family that you forget about God? Life goes by so fast. Days seem like weeks and weeks seem like months. All of a sudden, the busyness is all gone, and you are all alone. Try talking to an elderly person, they will tell you how quickly the years go.

It's a good idea to journal your life if you ever have some time on your hands. You will be surprised how your life will change when you compare year by year and what you accomplished in a particular time in your life.

God wants you to cast all your cares upon him and not worry about the future.

It's like an infant in the first few days of life; they don't have a care in the world, they rely on others to take care of them. Try letting God take care of you, starting today.

*****

Dear God,

Thank you for caring for me in this life. Guide me to share your love with others. Amen.

MAY 26

> For Christ also hath once suffered for sins, the just for the unjust, that he might bring us to God, being put to death in the flesh, but quickened by the Spirit. (1 Peter 3:18)

This passage speaks about exaltation and coming alive. Jesus died on the cross to take away your sins. You are redeemed and sanctified. Jesus made the sacrifice so you would not need to.

Focus your life on a new beginning or a new flesh. It's a great feeling to have your sins washed away.

God is asking you to go out and share his love with others. Any act of kindness is important in God's eyes. It is the thought that counts and God does notice your actions. Give God the glory.

How can you show love to those around you? Think about it seriously. If there was more love and kindness in the world, hatred and the devil would not exist. Be the positive image people look for in others.

*****

Dear God,

Thank you for coming alive in your spirit to me. Be with me and guide me to serve you for the rest of my life while I am on this earth. Amen.

MAY 27

> But ye are a chosen generation, a royal priesthood, an holy nation, a peculiar people; that ye should shew forth the praises of him who hath called you out of darkness into his marvelous light. (1 Peter 2:9)

You are among God's chosen people. Think about that! You are chosen by God. All God asks of you is to praise his holy name on high.

One way to praise God is by singing songs every week at church. The pastor preaches the gospel to you and inspires you to go out and make disciples of all nations.

God has no preference whether you share his love to one person or a group; just share His love with others. Let the minister inside you shine out with others today.

*****

Dear God,

Thank you for choosing me to be a child of yours. Be with me to shine out into the world and spread Your gospel to others. Amen.

MAY 28

> Every good gift and every perfect gift is from above, and cometh down from the Father of lights, with whom is no variableness, neither shadow of turning. (James 1:17)

This passage speaks about the source of blessings. Blessings as you serve the Lord. Blessings as you eat his food and drink his water. God sends rain to grow the seeds in the field to make the crops plentiful.

Remember God is the light of the world and shines down on you to provide you eternal life in heaven. Praising God through your voice proclaims the perfect gift of salvation.

Start praising God today with your prayers and supplications. God is listening to you. It's never too late to start. Give God the glory.

*****

Dear God,

Thank you for giving me the perfect gift: Jesus dying on the cross for my sins. Be with me and grant me your peace as I venture out into this world to share your love with others in your kingdom. Amen.

MAY 29

> For I the Lord thy God will hold thy right hand, saying unto thee, "Fear not; I will help thee." (Isaiah 41:13)

This verse speaks about Divine Protection to believers. God protects you under His wings and His truth shall be your shield from harm. God can protect you every day whatever circumstance arises. Just call upon him when you feel you are in an uncomfortable situation and wait for his response.

The verse also illustrates encouragement. His salvation will be with you today and always. As is mentioned in Matthew 14:27, "Be of good cheer; it is I; be not afraid."

You can always look up to God when you need help or are afraid. God hears your prayers and supplications and will respond to your requests.

Give God the praise and glory and watch as you reap the rewards of His love upon your life.

*****

Dear God,

Thank you for being my Divine Protector in life. Grant me grace to know and do your will while I am on this earth. Amen.

MAY 30

> But be ye doers of the word, and not hearers
> only, deceiving your own selves. (James 1:22)

This passage talks about being obedient. It also relates to good works to glorify God. You can glorify God in a number of ways, such as sing praises or songs during a church service or participate in a Bible study at your local church. Every time you praise God, it is an opportunity to share his love with others.

God warns you not to have careless hearing; you may be tempted by the devil. Watch your tongue and speak only God-pleasing words. God does know your thoughts and actions.

Remember that he wants you to have good self-esteem and not hateful thoughts or actions. By showing love to others, you are an enlightenment in God's eyes.

*****

Dear God,

Thank you for showing me your good works. Be with me and guide me to share your love with others. Amen.

MAY 31

> Grace to you, and peace, from God our
> Father and the Lord Jesus Christ. (Philemon 1:3)

God's grace is for you. It is freely given. It enables you to lead a simple life in service to God. It may be compared to a pastor's life, dedicated to serving the church and God. Are you willing to devote your life to God? May be a difficult question to ponder.

Pastors and teachers dedicate their lives to serving. They could be serving the church or school for thirty, forty, or fifty years. That is quite a commitment of service.

God only asks of you what you can handle. Won't you consider making a commitment to God? Even a small sacrifice is a good way to start. Maybe start your day every morning with a prayer for God to be with you and protect you during the day. And if you have a good day, try a different prayer the second day and so on. Soon, you will be talking to God every day or throughout the day. God's blessings on your commitment.

*****

Dear God,

Thank you for giving me your grace. Be with me as I make a commitment of daily prayer to you. Amen.

JUNE 1

> Thy word is a lamp unto my feet, and a light unto my path. (Psalm 119:105)

God's word is the light in your darkness. By studying God's word, it will direct you down a path of hope and faith. God's abounding love for you surpasses all understanding and keeps you in a safe and secure place.

What a reassurance knowing God is with you in your comings and goings throughout your life. Give God your utmost attention during your daily walk with him.

Starting every morning with devotion or prayer and then meditation puts your day in the right direction. If you have a good day or even if you don't, try ending your day also with a prayer thanking him for all that he did for you during the day. God is there for you. You are a blessing to God and to your family. Give God the glory.

*****

Dear God,

Thank you for giving me your lamp to guide my path in the right direction. Guide me to share your love with others in your kingdom. Amen.

JUNE 2

> O give thanks unto the Lord; for he is good:
> because his mercy endureth forever. (Psalm 118:1)

This is the table prayer that is often said after a meal. The prayer that is thanking God for his goodness and mercy. Do you thank God after the meal? The prayer that is thanking God for his goodness and mercy.

Thanking someone for doing a good deed for you or giving you a gift is the right thing to do. If you gave someone a gift, you would want them to respond the favor with a thank you.

Try starting each day with thanking God for giving you another day on this earth. The action will get your day off to a good start. After you thank God, then ask for his protection throughout the day. This small act will put positivity into your daily routine. God's blessings.

*****

Dear God,

Thank you for blessing me on a daily basis. Give me the strength to go into the world and serve you. Amen.

JUNE 3

> I will lift up mine eyes unto the hills, from whence cometh my help. My help cometh from the Lord, which made heaven and earth. (Psalm 121:12)

Looking upward to heaven for inspiration and help is what the passage is referring to. When you look up to heaven, you see the glory of God looking down on you. Oh, to know God loves you dearly.

God created the heaven and the earth. He can be described as the creator of the universe. He is credited for creating the sea and all things that are therein. What a marvelous God.

Take time to lift your heart up to God to thank him for giving you life, a family, and special friends in your life. His divine nature means he is the helper of people. Lay down your cares upon him and he will give you rest. God is good.

*****

Dear God,

Thank you for lifting my eyes up to the hills. You are my strength and comfort. Be with me as I spread Your gospel to others in your kingdom. Amen.

JUNE 4

> I was glad when they said unto me, Let us
> go into the house of the Lord. (Psalm 122:1)

This passage describes experiencing the love for God's house. Most people go to church on Sunday. What would happen if everyone went to church every day before they went to work? The pastors would be ecstatic. To have the church full every day would be a good problem to have. Of course, that is not actually possible since some people live in remote locations and distance would be a factor.

You could set up a small area in your house to worship God every day. Maybe a candle and a Bible. Starting each day in meditation with God could be a simple task then.

Try starting every day with the Lord in prayer. Your life will be enriched with numerous blessings.

*****

Dear God,

Thank you for sharing your love with me. Be with me to spread Your Word to others in your kingdom. Amen.

JUNE 5

> Our help is in the name of the Lord, who
> made heaven and earth. (Psalm 124:8)

The divine helper is God. He is with you in the morning when you wake up, throughout your day, and in the evening when you go to bed. He is there to support you when trials come into your life. He is with you to celebrate the successes you experience in your life and those of your family members.

It is a wonderful feeling knowing God is with you wherever you go. When you are feeling alone, take your request to God in prayer. He is there to comfort you.

Sometimes you may have a family member or friend who needs comforting; think of how God comforted you and extend care to that person. Sharing God's love to others is what life is all about. God's blessings to you.

*****

Dear God,

Thank you for being my divine helper. Guide me through this life to my eternal home. Help me share your love with others. Amen.

JUNE 6

> And being fully persuaded that, what he had promised, he was able also to perform. (Romans 4:21)

Some of God's divine abilities include fulfilling promises, making grace abound, giving exceedingly abundant joy, and to keep those from falling. This just demonstrates God's all-powerful nature. He is all-knowing and is there for you when you least expect it.

Turn yourself over to God and let him enter your life. You will be richly blessed by him. If you haven't started reading the Bible, this may be a good time to start.

Glorify God in his many blessings he has showered upon you. God is granting you eternal life. Take him into your life and watch your life prosper. God's blessings.

*****

Dear God,

Thank you for sharing your divine abilities with me. I am a poor, miserable sinner; grant me wisdom and peace to follow your path to eternal life. Amen.

JUNE 7

> For God is not unrighteous to forget your work and labor of love, which ye have shewed toward his name, in that ye have ministered to the saints, and do minister. (Hebrews 6:10)

Seeking love and happiness in the Lord means reinventing yourself as the new you. You may need to challenge yourself to overcome obstacles, which you have put off doing in the past.

In order to promote growth in your spiritual life, seek out Bible classes or small group studies at your church. You will be amazed what knowledge you can learn by discussing Bible passages with other Christians. Happiness will abound in your spiritual life as you read further into the Bible.

*****

Dear God,

Thank you for sharing your happiness with me. Give me your spirit to show happiness to others in this world. Amen.

JUNE 8

> The glory of young men is their strength:
> and the beauty of old men is the grey head.
> (Proverbs 20:29)

It is true that you are stronger when you are younger. As you age, your strength weakens, and bones become brittle.

Also with age comes gray hair. It is normal to get gray hair, sometimes more to seniors, but it also happens to middle-aged adults. The gray or white hair could also be a sign of maturity and wisdom. A senior citizen has experienced much in their life. They are always willing to share their wisdom with the younger generation.

The next time you encounter a senior citizen, ask them a question about their family or upbringing. They may be more than eager to share some of their life's journey they have experienced. God's blessings.

*****

Dear God,

Thank you for giving me strength throughout my life. Be with me on my journey to do your will and share your love with those around the world. Amen.

JUNE 9

> Trust in the Lord with all thine heart;
> and lean not unto thine own understanding.
> (Proverbs 3:5)

Trust is a powerful element. God wants you to put your trust in him with your whole heart. Giving God your full attention is what he is asking of you.

Do you give family members your undivided attention? Sometimes you get preoccupied and miss an important event because you thought you didn't need to attend. That event was special to your family member and probably made them very sad. The event may not happen again; think about the unhappiness you caused for that family member.

The next time an event happens, make every effort to attend, because it may not happen again. God's blessings.

*****

Dear God,

Thank you for putting trust in my life. Be with me to change my old habits and follow your example to love one another. Amen.

JUNE 10

> To everything there is a season, and a time to every purpose under the heaven: A time to be born, and a time to die; a time to plant, and a time to pluck up that which is planted. (Ecclesiastes 3:1–2)

As seasons go, there is a time to plant the seed and a time to harvest the crop. When water goes into the ground, it saturates the earth and is not able to get it back.

So it is with your life; sometimes you may say something unkind to someone and then regret it later. Words spoken cannot be retrieved.

God wants you to choose your words wisely and give them some thought before you speak them. Unkind words spoken can hurt people's feelings. Be considerate of others' feelings. God's blessings.

*****

Dear God,

Thank you for creating seasons. Be with me to carefully choose the words I use to share Your gospel with others. Amen.

JUNE 11

> A time to weep, and a time to laugh; a time
> to mourn, and a time to dance. (Ecclesiastes 3:4)

The seasons of life: weeping, laughing, mourning, and dancing.

Weeping and mourning tie in together and are familiar at death and at a funeral. You mourn for the loved one because you are going to miss seeing them. But thanks be to God, you will see them again in heaven.

Laughing is good for you and is a very healthy activity. Laughing is associated with jokes or a happy occasion. Laughing every day is the best medicine for you.

Dancing is a special skill that takes practice to perfect. Some people take dancing lessons to learn how to perfect their skill.

Try one of these activities (dancing or laughing) and see how your life changes for the better.

*****

Dear God,

Thank you for introducing laughter and dancing into my life. Be with me to learn how to improve my skill and share with others. Amen.

JUNE 12

> A time to cast away stones, and a time to gather stones together; a time to embrace, and a time to refrain from embracing. (Ecclesiastes 3:5)

There is a time for everything. God encourages you to show kindness to everyone. Be aware of unkind words that could hurt someone.

Instead, God encourages you to embrace one another with a hug. When was the last time you hugged a family member or a friend? Didn't it feel good?

On the other side of the scope, there is a time to refrain from embracing. An example, if someone said something to you and it hurt your feelings. You felt sad. That is the time to forgive that person and let them know the hurt it caused. God wants you to forgive one another.

It does take courage but finding that inner feeling to forgive may make you feel better on the inside.

*****

Dear God,

Thank you for showing kindness to me a poor, miserable sinner. Be with me and guide me to show more grace and mercy to those around me. Amen.

JUNE 13

> A time to get, and a time to lose; a time to
> keep, and a time to cast away. (Ecclesiastes 3:6)

In a ball game, it's not really the winning that counts—it's how you play the game. Not everyone wins; some lose the game. They give it their all, but one team seems to come out stronger. So it is in life; some people have better jobs and can afford nicer things in life. But are they really happy? As you go through life, take time to enjoy the important things like your family.

Life happens. Life happens very fast. Soon enough, years go by, and you may miss some of the important years when your family members were growing up. Don't have regrets by missing out on the opportunity to share those special moments with family.

There is a time to keep treasured gifts received from family and friends. Gifts are given to others out of love and compassion. If it's a keepsake, you may want to put it someplace special to always remember that person in the future.

Find a new tradition you can start to turn over a new leaf in your life to show God you truly do care about others. Even if you just bring one believer to Christ, it's a great start on your journey.

*****

Dear God,

Thank you for teaching me winning is not number one, but it's how you play the game. Guide me to show love and compassion to others in this world. Amen.

JUNE 14

> A time to rend, and a time to sew; a time to keep silence, and a time to speak. (Ecclesiastes 3:7)

A time to speak and a time to keep silent. Do you know those times? You speak when called upon at school or at a meeting at work. You may be asked your opinion or asked to answer a question. You speak freely and sometimes give your thoughts. God wants you to speak carefully and choose words appealing to others. Do not speak unkind words. That only makes people sad.

There is also a time to keep silent. When you were young and in class, and the teacher did the talking, it was your time to listen and learn. Then there would be a test shortly thereafter to see what you remembered in class. Or when you are with a group of people, it is best to let one person do the talking and everyone else listen to the conversation. If the person is giving instructions, it is even more important to listen, so you can follow the specific instructions for the task.

*****

Dear God,

Thank you for giving me the ability to talk and listen. Be with me and guide me to know the difference in life. Amen.

JUNE 15

> A time to love, and a time to hate; a time of
> war, and a time of peace. (Ecclesiastes 3:8)

A time to love. God wants you to love one another, just as he loves you. He is a loving God. Showing love to others is what this world is all about. Hatred sometimes is associated with war and nothing good ever comes from the harm it causes.

How do you show love to one another? Is it on a daily basis to your family and friends? Start today. Show love to one person, and then tomorrow show love to two people, and so on. Soon enough, you will be surprised at the good times you will share with others just by showing a little love and kindness to others.

Peace comes from getting along with others. Someone always needs to be the peacemaker in the group. If there is a disagreement among a number of people, there is usually one or two people who step up and try to settle the dispute so a resolution can be made.

Be the peacemaker in your family and set the example of showing love and compassion to others.

*****

Dear God,

Thank you for showing love to me as a sinner. Show me how to be a peacemaker to others in this world. Amen.

JUNE 16

> He hath made everything beautiful in his time: also he hath set the world in their heart, so that no man can find out the work that God maketh from the beginning to the end. (Ecclesiastes 3:11)

The works of God are wonderful. God shows that he is in control. He created the world from beginning to the end. Praise God for his marvelous works.

If it wasn't for God, there would be no creation. If it wasn't for your parents, you would not be on this earth. It is just amazing how life happens.

When it rains, it puts water in the fields for farmers and in gardens to make crops grow. When the sun shines, it helps the crops flourish. The winds provide the breeze to cool the days when the heat is too hot. God's work is all around us in his creation.

In your next prayer to God, thank him for creating the world. It is the reason you are on this earth.

*****

Dear God,

Thank you for making everything beautiful on this earth. Be with me to share your love with others. Amen.

JUNE 17

> For there is not a just man upon earth, that
> doeth good, and sinneth not. (Ecclesiastes 7:20)

Human imperfection is described in this passage. Everyone is a sinner and falls short of the glory of God. Jesus died on the cross to take away your sins. Thanks be to God there is salvation for us.

You may think you are perfect in this world, but God knows your faults and insecurities. He is always there to forgive you and give you a fresh start every day. Everyone makes mistakes in life, but by the grace of God, you are free to be children of God.

So the next time you see someone doing something wrong, do not say anything to them, God knows all things and is aware of the wrong. A similar wrong could happen to you. It's best to leave well enough alone and move on with your life.

*****

Dear God,

Thank you for making me whole and forgiving me for my imperfections. Be with me as I show love and kindness to others in this world. Amen.

JUNE 18

> Then I commended mirth, because a man hath no better thing under the sun, than to eat, and to drink, and to be merry: for that shall abide with him of his labor the days of his life, which God giveth him under the sun. (Ecclesiastes 8:15)

Every good gift comes from God. Enjoy your life in Christ. God warns you not to get caught up in the pleasures of life or carelessness of evil temptations.

Celebrating an event is a good thing; however, be wary of drinking excessively and the consequences it could lead to. So the next time you are invited to a joyous occasion, take heed and choose your fun carefully so it does not get out of hand.

As you start each new day, ask God to give you grace to continue on his path to eternal life.

*****

Dear God,

Thank you for giving me life in Jesus. Be with me to minister to others while I am here on this earth. Amen.

JUNE 19

> Thy word have I hid in mine heart, that I
> might not sin against thee. (Psalm 119:11)

God laid these words on your heart, and in your soul, and bound them for a sign upon your hand. God's Word is your faith. Believe that, and you will believe in the miracles God performs in you.

Singing songs and praises to God is showing love to one another. Every Sunday, you can hear the music and songs in church; what a joyous occasion to hear this marvelous noise.

God doesn't want you to hide your feelings in your heart; he wants you to open your heart and show others the love he gave you. Showing love to just one person today will spark the twinkle in someone's eye. You may have just made their day. Share God's love with one another.

*****

Dear God,

Thank you for sharing your miracles with me. Grant me grace to always show love to one another. Amen.

JUNE 20

> But God commendeth his love toward us,
> in that, while we were yet sinners, Christ died for
> us. (Romans 5:8)

Have you ever said an unkind word about someone? And then later regretted what you said? Afterward, the guilt you felt was overwhelming.

Jesus knows your thoughts and actions and forgives you when you have sinned and fallen short of the glory of God. Thanks be to God, his salvation sets you free. He died on the cross for your sins. You are now free to start a new day forgiven.

Each new day is a new start to your daily life. Just think, your sins are gone, and you are a new person. Jesus gives you the strength every day to tackle the world around you.

Remember you are a child of God and always in his protection wherever you may be.

*****

Dear God,

Thank you for loving me even though I am a sinner. Wrap your loving arms around me and give me your protection so that I may share my faith with others. Amen.

JUNE 21

> God is our refuge and strength, a very present help in trouble. Therefore will not we fear, though the earth be removed, and though the mountains be carried into the midst of the sea; though the waters thereof roar and be troubled, though the mountains shake with the swelling thereof. Selah. (Psalm 46:1–3)

God being your refuge and strength means having the confidence to go forward and defend yourself when in harm's way. You are ready to face adversities when they approach you. Self-confidence takes time and is earned over time. But once you have it, you can tackle whatever comes your way. No one can stand in your way.

Think of God as your divine helper—always there when you need to talk to someone in times of fear or tribulation. So when you are troubled, take your concerns to God in prayer. He is there to give you strength.

*****

Dear God,

Thank you for being my refuge and strength in my life. Guide me to follow your path of righteousness on my journey to eternal life. Amen.

JUNE 22

> And he that overcometh, and keepeth my works unto the end, to him will I give power over the nations. (Revelation 2:26)

God speaks about rewards bestowed upon those who overcome adversities in life.

Have you been in a difficult situation and struggled to find a resolution? You needed to make a decision based on a couple of options. Life is full of challenges, and it's up to you to choose the right option in the end.

If you choose the easier option, it may result in a wrong way. If you choose the harder option, it may result in the correct way but may take longer to accomplish.

Before you jump to conclusions, take your circumstance to God in prayer. He is there to listen to you and guide you in the right way. God is your comfort in time of trouble. Use your understanding wisely to make good decisions in the future. God's blessings.

*****

Dear God,

Thank you for helping me overcome obstacles in life. Be with me to share Your gospel with others and make the right decisions toward my path to eternal life. Amen.

JUNE 23

> When I consider thy heavens, the work of
> thy fingers, the moon and the stars, which thou
> hast ordained. (Psalm 8:3)

Worry, worry, worry. Everyone worries about life happenings. Try not to worry for today. How does that make you feel? Hopefully a lot happier than yesterday. When you speak from your heart, other happier emotions will occur.

Instead of worrying, try communicating your thoughts with others and do a good deed to encourage someone else's life.

A simple task like calling a friend you haven't spoken to in a while, shows that love to others that you care about them. Having lunch with a friend you haven't seen in quite some time, and catching up on old times, is always rewarding.

People are watching you, even when you may not realize it. As they say, always be on your best behavior. God's blessings.

*****

Dear God,

Thank you for helping me cope with my worrying habit. Help me to be a better person and share your love with others on this earth. Amen.

JUNE 24

> Now the Lord of peace himself give you peace always by all means. The Lord be with you all. (2 Thessalonians 3:16)

Peace comes in various forms. Some may include:

- when entering a house, you could say, "Peace be to this house."
- when you meet someone, you could say, "Peace be unto you."
- and as many as walk according to the rule, "Peace be unto them" (Galatians 6:16).
- greeting one another with a kiss of charity, "Peace be with you all that are in Christ Jesus" (1 Peter 5:14).

God doesn't care how you share peace with one another. The important point is sharing or showing peace with others.

Peace could be of a spiritual nature and linked with love, joy, gentleness, goodness, and faith. Have you thought of how you will share peace with others today? Give it some thought. Searching the scripture is a great start. Peace be unto you on your adventure.

*****

Dear God,

Thank you for sharing peace with me. Guide me to follow your command to share peace with mankind. Amen.

JUNE 25

> For we are saved by hope: but hope that is seen is not hope: for what a man seeth why doth he yet hope for? (Romans 8:24)

As you think about hope, also consider achieving that hope. Always looking for greater opportunities. You can hope for the better, but sometimes it takes a little longer for it to happen.

Achieving could be embracing your purpose in life and how you can help others. Your contributions may just be the needed assistance someone else was waiting for.

Consider the many blessings you enjoy every day. Look for ways to share your blessings with others around you.

*****

Dear God,

Thank you for your hope, joy, and peace. Be with me as I witness to others about the love of God. Amen.

JUNE 26

> Happy is that people, that is in such a case:
> yea, happy is that people, whose God is the Lord.
> (Psalm 144:15)

This passage refers to happiness as a tree of life. Holding on to gain strength or happiness in life.

What makes you happy in life? Is it your family, or maybe your job, or is it a positive attitude every day?

You are the only one responsible for your own happiness. How you live your life will affect your future. So give it some deep thought. Choose a lifestyle you are comfortable with. Don't try to live up to something you are not. Money can make your lifestyle comfortable but will it make you happy?

Take a step back and focus on where you see yourself in five or ten years. What can you imagine yourself doing in the future?

If you want to change your life, now is a good time to start. It's taking that first step. It may be a long step, but it will be worth it in the end.

*****

Dear God,

Thank you for putting happiness into my heart. Give me the strength and courage to continue on my happiness journey. Amen.

JUNE 27

> And he said unto them, Go ye into all the world, and preach the gospel to every creature. He that believeth and is baptized shall be saved; but he that believeth not shall be damned. (Mark 16:15–16)

This passage is referred to as, "The Great Commission." God wants his people to preach (or share) his word with others. You are encouraged to do mission work in your local community. Invite a friend or neighbor to attend church with you; or even better, offer to pick them up for church.

Taking someone to church with you may be a big deal for you. But for them, it could be that special part of their day. And the smile you put on their heart will be priceless.

If your friend tells you no at this time, give them some space or time. Maybe now is not the right time. Be patient. Wait for a few weeks and then ask them again to go with you to church. Don't give up. If the timing is not right, maybe it was not meant to be at this time. God is on your side and will give you the strength to conquer this task in the future.

*****

Dear God,

Thank you for sharing the Great Commission with me. Guide me to follow your instructions to share your love with others. Amen.

JUNE 28

> And he was withdrawn from them about
> a stone's cast, and kneeled down, and prayed.
> (Luke 22:41)

This passage speaks about a position for praying: kneeling. What position do you pray in?

It doesn't matter what position you pray in. The important part is that you are praying. Some other positions of praying include standing, sitting, or laying.

A prayer is a secret conversation between you and God. It's the conversation you have with God when you discuss intimate details of your life or how your day went. God is there to listen to your concerns.

He has a listening ear and will listen as long as it takes to voice your concern. Take your concerns to God and let him give you strength to face your challenges head on.

*****

Dear God,

Thank you for being patient with me as I take the time to pray. Give me the confidence to go to you in prayer whenever the need arises. Amen.

JUNE 29

> Let the word of Christ dwell in you richly in all wisdom; teaching and admonishing one another in psalms and hymns and spiritual songs, singing with grace in your hearts to the Lord. (Colossians 3:16)

This passage refers to the word of faith that is preached to all people. There are various means to hear God's Word. Some examples are hymns, spiritual songs, or singing with grace in your heart.

Singing is a wonderful means of using your voice to express praise to your Lord. It's never too late to start singing. Even the simplest songs can be a blessing to sing.

When you hear little children singing, it represents the joyous gifts they have to offer. As one of the favorite Bible passages says, "Let the little children come unto me," God encourages any age to come unto him with singing and praise.

Let your voice be heard. Consider how you can praise your Lord. It may be singing hymns or songs or even participating in a local choir. The sky is the limit. God's blessings.

*****

Dear God,

Thank you for the blessing of hymns and songs. Give me the guidance to start singing your praises more often. Amen.

JUNE 30

> In thee, O Lord, do I put my trust; let me never be ashamed: deliver me in thy righteousness. (Psalm 31:1)

Trust in God and be not ashamed. Trust can be linked with salvation and also strength in God. Where would you be without these? God provides many gifts to his people.

Having faith in God can go a long way. You may refer to your walk with God as a journey of faith. Not really a leap of faith but a slow path to finding out more about yourself and about God.

If you believe in yourself and are committed to a life of studying God's Word, you will be richly blessed many times over. God blesses his people by showing comfort and compassion every day to those who believe in him.

Why not start a life of service to God? A daily devotion or a meditation during the day is a good start. When you feel comfortable with your daily routine, tell friends, and maybe they may start a daily routine also. God's blessings.

*****

Dear God,

Thank you for putting your trust in me. I am a miserable sinner, and I need your daily forgiveness. Guide me so I stay on your path of righteousness. Amen.

JULY 1

> And the world passeth away, and the lust thereof: but he that doeth the will of God abideth forever. (1 John 2:17)

Everyone has dreams. Some dreams come true. God knows exactly what you are thinking and dreaming about.

Consider a future endeavor. Not sure how to tackle that task? Start small and work your way up to a little more involved task to see if it works for you. An example would be serving on a committee at church or school. When you feel more confident, the next time the task is presented, try serving as a cochair or offering to set up or cleanup. The people you meet while serving on a committee will be great to work with. You will reap the rewards during your time serving on a committee.

God will be your guide and show you the direction to go. Call upon God in every time of need.

*****

Dear God,

Protect me as I go about doing your work in Your kingdom. Guide me to start small and work my way upward toward a larger group. Amen.

JULY 2

> And I will give unto thee the keys of the kingdom of heaven: and whatsoever thou shalt bind on earth shall be bound in heaven: and whatsoever thou shalt loose on earth shall be loosed in heaven. (Matthew 16:19)

Keys of the kingdom is the second gift of Christ to believers. Various passages in the Bible refer to the keys as:

1. Keys to the House of David or key to David
2. Keys of hell and death or the bottomless pit (hell)

God gave us the keys since he has authority over heaven and earth. He wants you to be able to come to him freely and without reservation. His house is always open for you.

Open your heart and acknowledge God as the authority over heaven and earth and then let Jesus in to comfort you with his compassion. God's blessings.

*****

Dear God,

Thank you for providing me the key to your kingdom. Be with me to continue your work of bringing the lost to your eternal home. Amen.

JULY 3

> Behold, I give unto you power to tread on serpents and scorpions, and over all the power of the enemy: and nothing shall by any means hurt you. (Luke 10:19)

Power over evil spirits is the third gift of Christ to believers. God wants you to yield to temptation. Don't let the devil have any power over you. You are strong and can ward off any harm others cause you.

Be still in the Lord and ask for his protection. Trust in the Lord and keep your heart fixed on doing his will. God is your security and a help in need.

Read the Bible to find comfort in God's word. God does not want you to be afraid but believe in the hope of eternal life. It's a comforting truth to know God is with you all the time and will guide you through life's challenges. God grant you grace in His spirit.

*****

Dear God,

Thank you for watching over me when evil spirits come into my life. Be with me and strengthen me to do your will until my last breath. Amen.

JULY 4

> Shew thy marvelous lovingkindness, O thou that savest by thy right hand them which put their trust in thee from those that rise up against them. (Psalm 17:7)

This is a good Psalm to begin a prayer with. God is showing loving kindness to you, along with his mercy. He cleanses you from all your iniquities and sin.

In this Psalm, David prays to God for remission of his sins and for sanctification.

Do you ask God to forgive your sins? God's people sin on a daily basis. Asking God to take away your sins and blot out our transgressions is what He wants us to do.

Knowing you can start each day cleansed from all your wrongdoing is a good feeling. God looks down upon you and then showers you with his loving kindness as only he knows how to do.

*****

Dear God,

Thank you for showing me your loving kindness. Be with me and grant me grace to know and do your will. Amen.

JULY 5

> I am the living bread which came down from heaven: if any man eat of this bread, he shall live forever: and the bread that I will give is my flesh, which I will give for the life of the world. (John 6:51)

Bread of heaven is the fifth gift of Christ to believers. Jesus is the bread of life. He that cometh to thee shall never hunger. He giveth life into the world. Jesus wants you to believe in him.

This passage refers to bread that comes from heaven, and if you eat the bread, you shall live eternally.

Jesus wants you to study his word and be in the word. Take time to live your life as a faithful servant of God. Serving God with grace and mercy. Always looking to help others in His kingdom. Live a life of happiness and gratitude, and you'll go far in life.

*****

Dear God,

Thank you for giving me your living bread through Jesus. Continue to guide me to share your love with others. Amen.

JULY 6

> That they do good, that they be rich in good works, ready to distribute, willing to communicate. (1 Timothy 6:18)

When you were younger, you probably dreamed of what you wanted to do when you grew up. Have any of your dreams come true? When God created you, since He is all-knowing, He knew what you would do in the future.

If you don't have plans for the future, think about what you are good at; maybe what you went to college for isn't working out in the job world right now.

Trying a new adventure may just trigger a past dream you may have had. It's never too late to explore a new occupation or hob-by. New doors may open for you; take advantage of every opportunity presented to you. Life is too short; be adventurous.

*****

Dear God,

Thank you for being my creator. Guide me to show more good in the world to other. Amen.

JULY 7

> Thou wilt keep him in perfect peace, whose mind is stayed on thee: because he trusteth in thee. (Isaiah 26:3)

Legacy of peace is the seventh gift of Christ to believers. God gives his people the gift of peace. He strengthens them with the law of peace. The world would be so much better if peace was the focus.

Tribulation and war does exist and sometimes it is unpredictable. The devil tempts people and evil comes out of it resulting in harm and danger. God doesn't want your heart to be troubled, nor does He want you to be afraid.

God is all-powerful and will protect you, but you have to believe in him and obey his word. He knows you are not perfect; that is why He sent Jesus to take away your sins. What a wonderful gift Jesus gave that saves you from the devil.

You need to have faith in Christ that all things will work out for the good in your life. He believes in you; now you need to believe in Him.

*****

Dear God,

Thank you for your legacy of peace shown unto me. Be with me while I continue your legacy and show love to others in your kingdom. Amen.

JULY 8

> Be strong and of a good courage: for unto this people shalt thou divide for an inheritance the land, which I sware unto their fathers to give them. (Joshua 1:6)

Be strong in the grace that is in Christ Jesus. And be strong in the power of his might. Jesus wants you to have courage in whatever battles you are faced with.

Life is a daily challenge. You will be faced with many trials as you go through life. Some circumstances may be difficult. But stay strong in God's word to get through tribulations that come your way.

Focus your life on the cross and what it stands for. Jesus should be the center of your life. His saving grace is abundantly with you. As you face uncertainties in life, never lose focus in Christ Jesus or what He has done for you in your life.

*****

Dear God,

Thank you for keeping me strong and giving me the courage to show your love to others. Be with me and guide me to the path of your eternal life. Amen.

JULY 9

> The Lord bless thee and keep thee. The Lord make his face shine upon thee, and be gracious unto thee. The Lord lift up his countenance upon thee, and give thee peace. (Numbers 6:24–26)

This passage is spoken every Sunday in church as the pastor blesses the congregation to go in peace and share God's Word to His kingdom.

God is your watchman and is always there to protect you. He could be considered your guardian angel. He is looking down and watching your every move.

This passage also relates to finding favor with God; being in the divine nature with God. He has authority over heaven and earth. His powerful nature shines down from above to give His people strength to face life's challenges.

What a great feeling to be blessed by God every Sunday and then go out and witness to others about his love. God's blessings.

*****

Dear God,

Thank you for your blessing upon me, a poor, sinful being. Please continue to be my watchman and protector as I go out into the world and be your witness. Amen.

JULY 10

> Then was our mouth filled with laughter, and our tongue with singing: then said they among the heathen, the Lord hath done great things for them. The Lord hath done great things for us; whereof we are glad. (Psalm 126:2–3)

God wants you to be filled with great things, including laughter, spiritual joy, singing, and gladness.

Are you filled with God's great things? If you are, then you are a very happy person. Everyone should want to be happy in life. If not, it would be a very sad world.

God wants you to have a mind of a child—always discovering new things in life and being overjoyed to experience things for the first time in your life.

If you are around young ones, they usually have a lot of questions like how come, why, what does that mean? And once you stop and think of the answers, you will realize how simple life can be in their eyes. They have a whole world to experience ahead of them.

*****

Dear God,

Thank you for all the great things you provide for me. Grant me understanding to go out and share your great things with others in this world. Amen.

JULY 11

> For the earth shall be filled with the knowledge of the glory of the Lord, as the waters cover the sea. (Habakkuk 2:14)

This passage talks about worldwide missions. Going out into the world and preaching the gospel to all humans.

Everyone can be a missionary in God's kingdom. You don't need to be a called servant of God. Even young children can witness to others. Children can talk about Jesus at school or on the playground.

The task doesn't need to be complicated. Just simply tell people, "Jesus loves you." Oh, what a precious statement to someone who is maybe having a bad day. If it's someone you know, invite them to church or your house for a Bible study.

People like to receive attention. And you might just be that person who can open their heart to Jesus. God's blessings.

*****

Dear God,

Thank you for providing mission work to me and others around the world. Be with me as I minister to those around me about your salvation. Amen.

JULY 12

> Seek ye the Lord, all ye meek of the earth, which have wrought his judgment; seek righteousness, seek meekness: it may be ye shall be hid in the day of the Lord's anger. (Zephaniah 2:3)

This passage speaks about seeking the Lord. Seeking the Lord with all your heart and soul. Look for your strength from him. As it is written, in Luke 11:10, "For everyone that asketh receiveth; and he that seeketh findeth; and to him that knocketh it shall be opened."

God is a very generous God. He provides every opportunity for you to witness to others. Your task at hand is to share God's Word with others.

How will you start your mission work with God? Think about it. The world is out there waiting for your response.

Give it some thought. Mission work can be as simple as you can make it. Don't make it so difficult. God will guide you along the way. God's blessings.

*****

Dear God,

Thank you for giving me the opportunity to seek You. Your mercy is unmeasurable. Be with me and guide me so I may witness to others. Amen.

JULY 13

> Yet now be strong, O Zerubbabel, saith the Lord; and be strong, O Joshua, son of Josedech, the high priest; and be strong, all ye people of the land, saith the Lord, and work: for I am with you, saith the Lord of hosts. (Haggai 2:4)

This verse speaks about a ringing call to duty. Calling all people to be strong to do God's work of the land. Be strong in God's grace that is in Christ Jesus and in the power of his might. Stand firm in the faith of brotherly love.

What is your calling of strength in the Lord? Is it your strong faith? Is it singing praises in church? Or is it your leadership qualities you exemplify in your community or on church committees?

Whatever your gift is, God appreciates your work in His kingdom. Continue to profess his word in the work you are doing in his kingdom. God's blessings.

*****

Dear God,

Thank you for giving me the opportunity to answer your call to duty. I am only one person, but with many doing your work, we can accomplish the great task of winning souls for you in Your kingdom. Amen.

JULY 14

> Then he answered and spake unto me, saying, This is the word of the Lord unto Zerubbabel, saying, Not by might, nor by power, but by my spirit, saith the Lord of hosts. (Zechariah 4:6)

This passage talks about the true means of success. Weapons are not needed. People can be powerless due to sin and unbelief. God provides spiritual power to give the courage to rebuke sin and the devil. God's spiritual power is mightier than physical force upon men.

What is your means of success? Do you have a strong spiritual power within you to conquer sin when the devil tempts you or you get into a dangerous situation? You can always turn to God for protection.

He is your guiding light when darkness comes upon you. God is your strength and hope in whatever situation arises. Call upon him and he will give you refuge.

*****

Dear God,

Thank you for giving me the courage to face harm when the devil comes near to me. Be with me and guide me through harm and danger until I reach my heavenly home with you. Amen.

JULY 15

> Ask and it shall be given you; seek, and ye shall find; knock, and it shall be opened unto you. For everyone that asketh receiveth; and he that seeketh findeth; and to him that knocketh it shall be opened. (Matthew 7:7–8)

This scripture speaks about the three-fold promise. God gives you strength to do his will. Another similar passage is in John 15:7, "If ye abide in me, and my words abide in you, ye shall ask what ye will, and it shall be done unto you."

The power of prayer plays a role in your life. Asking for something through prayer is a simple task. But the response may be long or short. God answers prayer. It could be right away or maybe not at this time. When it comes to prayer with God, it takes patience. Asking for forgiveness may be different than asking for protection from harm or danger. Be cautious in your prayer requests. God does hear your concerns and promises to answer them. God's blessings.

*****

Dear God,

Thank you for the power of prayer. Guide me to go to you whenever I am faced with a difficult situation in life. Amen.

JULY 16

> That if thou shalt confess with thy mouth the Lord Jesus, and shalt believe in thine heart that God hath raised him from the dead, thou shalt be saved. (Romans 10:9)

This passage refers to God's plan of salvation. Encouraging you to have a saving faith in Christ. If you believe, you will have eternal life. By hearing God's word and then believing, you shall have eternal life.

Jesus is your resurrection and life; if you believe in him, yet shall you live.

How do you confess your salvation? Are you an introvert or an extrovert when it comes to sharing God's love with others? It all depends on what is in your heart. God knows what you are thinking. Your confession is between you and God. As you make your confession to God, think of how it will affect your future.

*****

Dear God,

Thank you for sharing your plan of salvation with me. Please guide me to follow in your footsteps when sharing your love with others. Amen.

JULY 17

> Notwithstanding in this rejoice not, that the spirits are subject unto you; but rather rejoice, because your names are written in heaven. (Luke 10:20)

This scripture refers to the real reason for joy. Here are some familiar phrases you may have heard:

- rejoicing in the Lord always
- singing his praises from the mountaintops
- raise your voices and proclaim his glory

God has your name written in heaven. Someday you will be there to see it. As you have heard, Jesus is preparing a place for you in heaven. Are you ready? Some people's time to go to heaven is sooner than others.

You may think you have plenty of time left, or you may have things you want to do in life yet. Only God knows when your time is up. While you are busy living life, start preparing for heaven. Spend time with your loved ones. Tell family that you love them. Make every waking hour count, as if it was your last one. God's blessings.

*****

Dear God,

Thank you for putting joy in my life. Grant me the peace of understanding, so when my last hour is at hand, I may be prepared for eternal life in heaven. Amen.

JULY 18

> If ye abide in me, and my words abide in you, ye shall ask what ye will, and it shall be done unto you. (John 15:7)

Like this verse speaks about the master key of prayer. "Abide in God." A branch that cannot bear fruit by itself, but abides by the vine, so you accept God's guidance. You also look to God while keeping his commandments. What a wonderful reflection of God's love.

God also wants you to have confidence in sharing his love and not be ashamed to speak to others about the word of God.

How are you abiding in God's word? Are you sharing his love to mankind? Remember, sometimes your actions speak louder than your words. So always be cautious of your actions around others.

*****

Dear God,

Thank you for abiding in me. Grant me understanding to abide in your wisdom and share your love with others. Amen.

JULY 19

> Take therefore no thought for the morrow: for the morrow shall take thought for the things of itself. Sufficient unto the day is the evil thereof. (Matthew 6:34)

This passage speaks of taking away stress. You should not worry about what you should eat or drink or what you should wear. God wants you to think of how you live your life. Don't worry about material things.

As 1 Peter 5:7 speaks of "Casting all your care upon him: for he careth for you," give all your cares to God in prayer.

God does not want you to worry. Go on with your life in a positive way, knowing all your cares are given to God.

Just think of how good it will feel to unload all your worries off your shoulders. Letting go of unimportant issues allows you to concentrate on other more important ones at hand. God's blessings.

*****

Dear God,

Thank you for taking stress out of my life. Guide me to focus more on loving you and sharing Your gospel with others in your kingdom. Amen.

JULY 20

> For other foundation can no man lay than that is laid, which is Jesus Christ. (1 Corinthians 3:11)

The other foundation is the spiritual foundation which is Jesus Christ. Building a firm foundation on Jesus assures you of eternal life.

When you build a house, the foundation is the base and holds everything else up for the house. Selecting a good contractor to build your house is critical, so your house lasts for many years to come.

So it is true with building your faith on a firm foundation with God as the base and adding to it to make your faith strong.

How are you building your faith foundation? Is Jesus your base? When building your foundation, consider having faith and hope and joy added into your life to make it complete.

Start today. Building your foundation to secure your place in God's kingdom. God's blessings.

*****

Dear God,

Thank you for giving me your spiritual foundation in Christ. Give me a true spirit to focus on loving others in Your kingdom. Amen.

JULY 21

> For God, who commanded the light to shine out of dark-ness, hath shined in our hearts, to give the light of the knowledge of the glory of God in the face of Jesus Christ. (2 Corinthians 4:6)

This passage refers to the illuminated heart. You need light to shine in your heart to welcome the word of God inside. The word is known to believers in Christ.

Christ is the light of the world. He is your redeemer, and as long as you know your redeemer lives, you have eternal life.

Do you let your light shine among those around you? Are you illuminating your faith to others? Stop and think what would be a good way to start letting your light shine in the world.

You may want to start by living a life of faith and hope. Soon others will see your change and may ask what has changed in your life. Be ready to tell them!.

*****

Dear God,

Thank you for being the light in my world. Your brightness and mercy are a welcome sign in my life. Amen.

JULY 22

> I am crucified with Christ: nevertheless I live; yet not I, but Christ liveth in me: and the life which I now live in the flesh I live by the faith of the Son of God, who loved me, and gave himself for me. (Galatians 2:20)

The scripture talks about dying with Christ. The saving faith of Christ lives within you. Open up your heart to let Christ's love inside you. The sacrifice on the cross was made for everyone in the world. Even though you are a sinner, Christ's love is for everyone on this earth.

Count your blessings and be glad you have a savior who loves you. Start today by letting Christ in your life.

A simple devotion every day is all you need to get started. A small prayer also will get your day off to a good start. God's blessings.

*****

Dear God,

Thank you for the saving faith of Christ shown upon me. Guide me to follow the path of righteousness to my eternal home in heaven. Amen.

JULY 23

> Till we all come in the unity of the faith, and of the knowledge of the Son of God, unto a perfect man, unto the measure of the stature of the fulness of Christ. (Ephesians 4:13)

This verse talks about the unity of Christ. You are all partakers of one bread, not individuals of one bread or one body. You are in unity with all believers. You strive to be perfect in Christ; to be Christlike. Your focus is being in the fullness of Christ.

What do you strive for in your belief of Christ? Do you have certain beliefs and share them with others? Sharing God's love with others is what God wants you to do. This verse relates to the Christian maturity and where you are in your faith journey.

Your faith journey is personal. You may be more comfortable starting with a daily devotion and private prayer with God. Or you may be more daring and join a Bible study group with your church family.

Make today the start of something new in your life and surprise yourself as your faith grows.

*****

Dear God,

Thank you for giving me unity of Christ and faith. Be with me as I follow you in my journey to eternal life with you. Amen.

JULY 24

> If ye then be risen with Christ, seek those things which are above, where Christ sitteth on the right hand of God. (Colossians 3:1)

This passage refers to being heavenly minded. You should be reaching for the higher calling of God when you seek God's love and affection.

The passage also talks about Christ being exalted and sitting on the right hand of God with all his power and majesty. You can look up to God to receive strength, honor, glory, blessing, and wisdom. These gifts are yours as a child of God.

Take one of the gifts and apply it to your life. It can be as simple as going to church or helping out a neighbor with an errand. Do something kind and thoughtful for someone today. Go out of your way to show that small bit of empathy to someone who may just need that joy in their heart today.

*****

Dear God,

Thank you for showing me how to be heavenly minded in my life. Grant me strength to share your love with others. Amen.

JULY 25

> For even when we were with you, this we commanded you, that if any would not work, neither should he eat. (2 Thessalonians 3:10)

This verse refers to the duty of labor. When you work and put forth effort, then you can eat. You can also afford to buy clothes and material things for yourself and your house. If you do not work, then money does not come in.

If would be difficult making a living without income to support yourself. There are circumstances that may prevent you from working, such as disability or an illness. Some individuals only work part-time, and that's okay; it's still a small amount of money coming in.

Working at a job gives value to your life. It lifts your self-confidence and self-esteem.

You feel that your life is worth something when you can provide for your family. God encourages you to labor in His kingdom and serve others.

*****

Dear God,

Thank you for providing me with the duty of labor. Be with me as I work in your kingdom. Amen.

JULY 26

> Who gave himself for us, that he might redeem us from all iniquity, and purify unto himself a peculiar people, zealous of good works. (Titus 2:14)

This passage talks about the Redeemer's purpose, laying down his life for all people. He washed us from our sins with his own blood.

God's redemption for us and cleansing of the Holy Spirit results in your freedom from your sins. God wants you to do good works for others to show the love he shows to you.

Are you purified in God's love? Do you feel his power upon you? His mighty good works are all around you. Just look at creation and you will see what great things he has created for his people.

*****

Dear God,

Thank you for giving me the Redeemer's purpose in life. Be with me and guide me on my journey to everlasting life. Amen.

JULY 27

> Let him know, that he which converteth the sinner from the error of his way shall save a soul from death and shall hide a multitude of sins. (James 5:20)

This passage talks about the soul winner's achievement, his beloved son. He delivered you from the power of darkness and hath translated you into his kingdom.

God shows you his knowledge in this passage reflecting on how He will lay down His life for His sheep.

This is how parents feel about their children. They want the best for them and will often go out of their way to provide the best for them.

Thank your parents for the great job they did in raising you. You are their child and also a child of God. Just remember how special you are in their eyes.

God hears your requests, so be cautious what you ask for. It may be better to listen; then talk. It's up to you to decide the importance of the topic.

*****

Dear God,

Thank you for sending me your beloved son, Jesus. He has provided much love to me. Be with me and show me the way on my journey to everlasting life. Amen.

JULY 28

> Forasmuch as ye know that ye were not redeemed with corruptible things, as silver and gold, from your vain conversation received by tradition from your fathers; But with the precious blood of Christ, as of a lamb with-out blemish and without spot. (1 Peter 1:18–19)

These verses speak about the cost of redemption. It comments on: gold, silver, old life (bought you back from sin), traditions, parental influence, and the blood of Christ.

You were redeemed by the precious blood of Christ, without blemish and without spots. Without blemish can be related to a glorious church; not having any spot or wrinkle, but rather being holy like the Holy Spirit.

This passage also speaks of Christ being sinless and with no guile coming from his mouth. How can God's people follow this example? You sin every day and fall short of his mercy. You are influenced by the evil happenings in this world.

*****

Dear God,

Thank you for redeeming me, a lost and condemned soul. Lead me on the right path to bring others into Your kingdom. Amen.

JULY 29

> And this is love, that we walk after his commandments. This is the commandment, That, as ye have heard from the beginning, ye should walk in it. (2 John 1:6)

This verse speaks of love and obedience. Christ commands you to keep his commandments as you live your life. When you walk in truth and obey his law, you are showing him love and respect.

How many times have you tried to keep his commandments but then get tempted by the devil? You may get tempted by the lusts of the world or by others telling you it's a good thing to do, but then it is really not in the long run.

Obeying God and keeping his commandments is a hard thing to do. Trying to do the right thing every day can truly be a struggle.

Try focusing on what the right thing is to do is even though it may be difficult at times. Ask God to give you guidance along the way, and you will be surprised how the end result will be a lot better for you than being tempted by the devil to do wrong.

*****

Dear God,

Thank you for giving me your commandments and your love. Please forgive me when I do wrong. Give me the courage to stand up to evil foes and to have the confidence to face challenges head on. Amen.

JULY 30

> Now unto him that is able to keep you from falling, and to present you faultless before the presence of his glory with exceeding joy, To the only wise God our Savior, be glory and majesty, dominion and power, both now and ever. (Jude 1:24–25)

This passage refers to a divine keeper. Other names may be the pilgrim's companion, the sleepless watchman, the protecting father or the Almighty Guardian. His divine presence and divine acts are all around you.

Some of the traits referring to God are glorifying God, salvation of God, God's majesty, God's power, and God is eternal.

As you research more in the Bible, it is amazing the knowledge you learn and just how amazing God is in this world. God is faultless. You may try to be sinless, but the devil is always there trying to bring you down. Keep your focus on God, and your life will be well-lived and happy.

*****

Dear God,

Thank you for being my divine keeper and my protecter through life. Keep me strong in Your Word, so I may keep on the path to eternal life. Amen.

JULY 31

> Fear thou not; for I am with thee: be not dismayed; for I am thy God: I will strengthen thee; yea, I will help thee; yea, I will uphold thee with the right hand of my righteousness. (Isaiah 41:10)

This verse talks about God's divine presence. His strength is promised to his people. He promises to be the divine helper and divine supporter when His people need him.

What a wonderful, comforting verse knowing God is there for you, with his right hand supporting you through every trial and tribulation you may experience.

Just having God near you when you are having a tough day can be the reassurance you need to get you through the day.

Try starting and ending every day with God in prayer. Your life will be enriched beyond measure. God's blessings.

*****

Dear God,

Thank you for your divine presence in my life. Give me the strength and courage to continue on my journey to eternal life. Amen.

AUGUST 1

> But Jonah rose up to flee unto Tarshish from the presence of the Lord and went down to Joppa; and he found a ship going to Tarshish: so he paid the fare thereof, and went down into it, to go with them unto Tarshish from the presence of the Lord. (Jonah 1:3)

Do you ever find that you may be going the wrong way than you should have gone? It could be an expensive journey on your part.

Everyone makes wrong choices in life. It's just a part of living. It's the choices you make, however, that determine your future.

If you are faced with a challenging situation, ask God for guidance. Take your time so you don't make a hasty decision. It's important to make the right decision in the long run. God's blessings.

*****

Dear God,

Thank you for showing me the right way to do things in life. Life is full of obstacles and challenges. Be with me to follow your path to eternal life. Amen.

AUGUST 2

> Shall I not in that day, saith the Lord, even destroy the wise men out of Edom, and understanding out of the mount of Esau? (Obadiah 1:8)

This passage refers to humbling of the proud. This occurs after destruction of Edom.

God's people are sometimes too proud of their status in life and find it difficult to humble themselves to reality. God doesn't want people to be buoyant and wicked. He wants his people to have a humble attitude and treat others with kindness and respect.

Think of a humbling experience you may have had in the past. How did it make you feel? Remember to keep focused on the cross when life gets to be challenging. God is there for you.

*****

Dear God,

Thank you for keeping me humble in your kingdom. Be with me to show love to others I meet in life. Amen.

AUGUST 3

> Behold, the days come, saith the Lord God, that I will send a famine in the land, not a famine of bread, nor a thirst for water, but of hearing the words of the Lord. (Amos 8:11)

This verse talks about the spiritual famine. It's not about food or water but listening to God's word.

This ties in to going to church on a regular basis. Getting involved in Bible classes or Bible study groups. Or you could even use daily meditation to focus on God's word.

It really doesn't matter what form of study you participate in—just taking the first step is the most important. Talk to people and get an idea of what others are doing to hear the word of God. It takes time to compile your ideas. God will guide you on how to get started. God's blessings.

*****

Dear God,

Thank you for guiding me in the right direction to hearing God's word. Continue to lead me down the path of righteousness for Your Name's sake. Amen.

AUGUST 4

> And it shall come to pass afterward, that I will pour out my spirit upon all flesh; and your sons and your daughters shall prophesy, your old men shall dream dreams, your young men shall see visions. (Joel 2:28)

This passage speaks about the outpouring of the spirit. Everyone has dreams and visions. It could be dreams of what you would like to be in the future, or it could be a vision of how you want a particular project to develop in the future.

There is nothing wrong with visions or dreams. Just don't get carried away and think they will all happen. Coming back to reality puts things in perspective.

So the next time you have a dream, ask yourself, "Could this be true or is it just a dream?" Knowing the difference between dreams and reality is half the battle. God's blessings.

*****

Dear God,

Thank you for giving me your outpouring spirit. Keep me in your protection and guide me to stay on your path to everlasting life. Amen.

AUGUST 5

> Then shall we know, if we follow on to know the Lord: his going forth is prepared as the morning; and he shall come unto us as the rain, as the latter and former rain unto the earth. (Hosea 6:3)

This verse speaks of the road to divine blessing. The blessing of loving kindness, judgment, and righteousness in the earth. Jesus wants people to continue in his word and be his disciples.

He has prepared the way for you and wants you to believe in him that he is the only true God. God's grace is showered upon his people. Take time to relish his faith and hope that he offers through your church. Churches offer a variety of worship gatherings or Bible studies.

Make it a priority to start some sort of Bible study within the next week. God's blessings on your new adventure.

*****

Dear God,

Thank you for sharing your divine blessing with me. Guide me to continue following in your spirit down the path to eternal life. Amen.

AUGUST 6

> Now when Daniel knew that the writing was signed, he went into his house; and his windows being open in his chamber toward Jerusalem, he kneeled upon his knees three times a day, and prayed, and gave thanks before his God, as he did aforetime. (Daniel 6:10)

This passage speaks about the consistent habit of prayer. Prayer can be in any form and at any time or in any position. The act of praying is the most important. God hears all your prayers and encourages you to pray often.

Maybe you do have a prayer ritual you follow every day. If not, you may want to start and let God into your life. A prayer can be one or two sentences. Keep it simple.

God wants you to open up to him with prayer. After all, he is your father in heaven. Let him shower you with his grace and might.

*****

Dear God,

Thank you for putting prayer in my life. Guide me to continue my prayer life and show love to others in Your kingdom. Amen.

AUGUST 7

> It is of the Lord's mercies that we are not consumed, because his compassions fail not. (Lamentations 3:22)

This scripture speaks about God's unfailing mercies. His mercy is boundless and reaches beyond the clouds. He forgives the sins of his people.

Where else can you find a God who makes salvation possible for all people? God is gracious to you, is slow to anger, and shows kindness to all.

The next time you are faced with a difficult situation, think of God's mercy he has shown to you. God goes above and beyond to care for his people. Look up to God in prayer when life's struggles are overwhelming. God is your saving grace and your Redeemer. Cast all your cares upon him for he cares for you.

*****

Dear God,

Thank you for your unfailing mercy you have shown to me. Protect me from the evil one and guide me along your path of righteousness. Amen.

AUGUST 8

> And ye shall seek me, and find me, when ye shall search for me with all your heart. (Jeremiah 29:13)

This passage talks about the greatest discovery, Jesus. If you seek, you will find him. Jesus is your reward. What a find! Some people search their entire life and never find Jesus. If you have laid down your life and found Jesus as your Savior, you are one of the blessed ones.

You know your Redeemer lives. You have salvation! Now it's time to tell others about the love of Jesus so they can be saved. Share how he has saved you and can save them also.

What is your game plan? If you start today, you may find some of the lost and erring. God is on your side, just ask him for guidance. God's blessings.

*****

Dear God,

Thank you for sending Jesus to die on the cross for my sins. Continue guiding me on the path to righteousness until I reach my heavenly home. Amen.

AUGUST 9

> For unto us a child is born, unto us a son is given: and the government shall be upon his shoulder: and his name shall be called Wonderful, Counsellor, the Mighty God, the Everlasting Father, the Prince of Peace. (Isaiah 9:6)

This passage talks about the most wonderful child, Jesus. These are some of the very descriptive names for Jesus:

- Wonderful—means miracle
- Counsellor—means advisor
- The mighty God—means He is God
- The everlasting Father—means he made you and forgives you
- The Prince of Peace—means *Prince* which gives peace

Oh, to have the wisdom from above shine down upon you and give you peace.

Treasure your name your parents gave you. You were their chosen child. Find out the meaning of your name. It was a special name they chose just for you. Thank God every day for bringing you into this world, because you are very special indeed.

*****

Dear God,

Thank you for sending Jesus into my life. Help me to show love to others as you have loved me. Amen.

AUGUST 10

> Let us hear the conclusion of the whole matter: Fear God and keep his commandments: for this is the whole duty of man. (Ecclesiastes 12:13)

This scripture talks about the greatest conclusion, keeping his commandments. By keeping his commandments, you should "fear the Lord thy God, to walk in all his ways, and to love him and to serve the Lord thy God with all thy heart and with all thy soul" (Deuteronomy 10:12).

That is a very tall order of duties to fulfill.

- Do you fear the Lord?
- Do you walk in his ways?
- Do you love him?
- Do you serve him?

How many of these questions did you say yes to?

If you want to keep his commandments, you may want to start your duties today. Put Christ in your life and discover the abundance of joy you will experience. He is there for you every step of the way.

*****

Dear God,

Thank you for giving me your commandments to follow. Be with me as I start my life today keeping your commandments. Amen.

AUGUST 11

> But one thing is needful: and Mary hath chosen that good part, which shall not be taken away from her. (Luke 10:42)

Are you like Mary? Have you chosen that which is right?

People are busy with their lives and forget to stop and take in the moment. Life is too short, so don't miss an important event in your life. Take in everything life has to offer. Live life and create memories with your family and friends.

God put you on this earth for a purpose. Find that purpose. Give 100 percent of yourself every day. Don't delay what you can do today. Tomorrow may never come.

Make Christ the center of your life. He alone has reserved a place for you in heaven with him. God's blessings.

*****

Dear God,

Thank you for choosing me to be your child on earth. Grant me grace and understanding to continue living Your Word through the Bible, until I reach my heavenly home. Amen.

AUGUST 12

> And the Lord turned the captivity of Job,
> when he prayed for his friends: also the Lord gave
> Job twice as much as he had before. (Job 42:10)

This passage talks about the enriching prayer. Job was rewarded with twice as much as he had before. What a tremendous gesture or "generosity" by God.

Do you ever say a prayer and receive something you never thought was possible? It makes you very surprised and happy. That's what life is all about, making someone's day. Surprising them with a gesture when they least expect it.

Why not make someone in your life very happy. Surprise them with something they never expected. And then wait for their reaction. It really makes you feel good when you make someone feel special. God's blessings.

*****

Dear God,

Thank you for providing prayer in my life. Prayer is a powerful tool and provides miracles when you least expect it. Grant me grace and wisdom to continue on my prayer journey. Amen.

AUGUST 13

> For Ezra had prepared his heart to seek the law of the Lord, and to do it, and to teach in Israel statutes and judgments. (Ezra 7:10)

This scripture talks about the faithful scribe. Ezra prepared his heart spiritually for the Lord. This task involves abandoning idols, cleansing, and then personal purification unto the Lord.

How do you prepare for the Lord? Look inside your heart and be sincere about your faith. Are you obedient to the Lord? When you were young, you obeyed your parents. In a similar way, obey God.

God will accept your heart any way you open it up to him. Be honest with yourself. God is gracious with you and very understanding. God's blessings.

*****

Dear God,

Thank you for giving me a faithful heart. Please keep my spirit in your hope and love until I reach my heavenly home. Amen.

AUGUST 14

> I can do all things through Christ which strengtheneth me. (Philippians 4:13)

God promises to give you strength when you least expect it. It could be strength in a battle you are experiencing or a situation where you need to make a tough decision.

God makes you strong to face challenges in your life. As mentioned in Isaiah 40:31, "But they that wait upon the Lord shall renew their strength; they shall mount up with wings as eagles; they shall run, and not be weary; and they shall walk, and not faint."

That is quite the energy God provides you. You may think you are tired, but he recharges you to go the extra mile.

Just remember the next time you get tired and don't want to go any further, God is there next to you giving you the strength to keep going until the end. Enjoy your journey with the Lord.

*****

Dear God,

Thank you for giving me strength. Strength to finish the battle of life until I reach my eternal home. Amen.

AUGUST 15

> For the eyes of the Lord run to and fro throughout the whole earth, to shew himself strong in the behalf of them whose heart is perfect toward him. Herein thou hast done foolishly: therefore from henceforth thou shalt have wars. (2 Chronicles 16:9)

This scripture speaks about the all-seeing eye. God's power and strength rules the earth. He sees what goes on in everyone's lives.

Even if a person does something foolish in God's eyes, He is aware of the action. And sometimes wars do occur because of unruly circumstances. Wars cause death and destruction to communities and towns. It is not a good thing. God encourages unity and peace among his people. He is love.

*****

Dear God,

Thank you for being my all-seeing eye. Please keep me in your protection as I am on my journey through life. Amen.

AUGUST 16

> And Jabez called on the God of Israel, saying, Oh that thou wouldest bless me indeed, and enlarge my coast, and that thine hand might be with me from evil, that it may not grieve me! And God granted him that which he requested. (1 Chronicles 4:10)

This verse talks about a wonderful prayer in dark surroundings. Have you ever been in an uncomfortable situation and called out to God in prayer for protection?

At some point in life, you may be faced with the devil. How will you handle it? God wants you to pray about it. He will hear you. He will answer your prayer. Maybe not the same day; it may be later in time. God encourages you to be patient and have faith in him. His divine hand will protect you when you need him the most.

Give God a chance to show his righteousness upon you and give you strength.

*****

Dear God,

Thank you for protecting me in the darkest hour of my life. Be with me and grant me grace as I go through life and then be with you in heaven someday. Amen.

AUGUST 17

> Give therefore thy servant an understanding heart to judge thy people, that I may discern between good and bad: for who is able to judge this thy so great a people? (1 Kings 3:9)

This verse is a prayer for wisdom. Everyone needs wisdom in their life. Knowing the good from the bad and using your best judgment to make the right choice.

If your decision is not a good one, there may be consequences. And you have to live with the outcome. An example may be, you purchased an older home because it was less money. However, it takes time and money for remodeling and replacing appliances could turn out to be a financial burden in the long run. It's a decision you made, but you felt it was the best decision at the time. God understands people are faced with circumstances and need to react too quickly sometimes. Take time to think out your decisions and not hastily jump to conclusions. God is patient with you.

*****

Dear God,

Thank you for giving me wisdom and understanding. Grant me peace to follow your direction in life until I reach my heavenly home. Amen.

AUGUST 18

> Yea, though I walk through the valley of the shadow of death, I will fear no evil: for thou art with me; thy rod and thy staff they comfort me. (Psalm 23:4)

As life goes on, there are times you travel through the darkest valley. The valley may be the loss of a close relative or friend. Death (for the ones left behind) is sometimes a struggle.

God comforts you with His love. Reading the Bible provides comfort and understanding. Knowing that God provides His unconditional love is your assurance of eternal life.

The next time you experience the darkest valley, embrace His word and wait for his guidance and direction.

May you be blessed with a spiritual life and fruitfulness.

*****

Dear God,

Thank you for comforting me while in the darkest valley. Be with me and provide guidance as I walk in your ways. Amen.

AUGUST 19

> And Ruth said, Intreat me not to leave thee, or to return from following after thee: for whither thou goest, I will go; and where thou lodgest, I will lodge: thy people shall be my people, and thy God my God. (Ruth 1:16)

This verse is a shining example of constancy. Friendships are constant. A true friend is always there for you when you need them.

Are you a true friend? What would your friends say about you? To have a friend, you have to be a friend. Think about that statement. It's a powerful statement.

As the song goes, "What a friend we have in Jesus." Start being a friend to someone in need. It's a good feeling to have a friend when it is really needed.

Go forth and be a witness of your faith to those around you.

*****

Dear God,

Thank you for being a shining example of constancy in my life. Grant me peace and give me protection on my journey through life. Amen.

AUGUST 20

> And she said, The Philistines be upon thee, Samson. And he awoke out of his sleep, and said, I will go out as at other times before, and shake myself. And he wist not that the Lord was departed from him. (Judges 16:20)

This verse speaks about the lost power. Samson was mighty in physical strength, yet weak in resisting temptation.

Does that happen in your life? You think you can handle any situation that arises, but then you are taken back by reality and your conscience says otherwise. For example, you are part of a group sponsoring an event; everyone has a part to do and all of a sudden the electricity goes out in the facility. You need to make fast decisions before guests arrive for the event.

This does happen, and it is unfortunate for the people sponsoring the event. The time and money that goes into the planning and then the relocating or rescheduling comes into play. Being flexible is what life is all about. God is with you all the way. Don't be afraid to call on him in times of trouble for guidance.

*****

Dear God,

Thank you for giving me physical strength. Please guide me also to have the knowledge not to be weak when times get tough. Amen.

AUGUST 21

> This book of the law shall not depart out of thy mouth; but thou shalt meditate therein day and night, that thou mayest observe to do according to all that is written therein: for then thou shalt make thy way prosperous, and then thou shalt have good success. (Joshua 1:8)

The price of success is inevitable. Focus on wise thoughts as you experience difficulties in life. Meditate on God's word when life gets tough. Do not be tempted by the devil and evil thoughts.

God wants you to read the Bible day and night. This may be a tall order to accomplish. Take one day at a time.

It's starting a new task that is always the hardest. God's blessings.

*****

Dear God,

Thank you for putting wise thoughts into my heart. Your wisdom is what I need in my life. Grant me peace to overcome the devil and temptations of the world. Amen.

AUGUST 22

> For God so loved the world, that he gave his only begotten Son, that whosoever believeth in him should not perish, but have everlasting life. (John 3:16)

God loves you. He showed you his love by sending Jesus to die on the cross to take away your sins.

How can you show love to others? First, start to love yourself. People do notice when you are happy and loving. Second, show love and kindness to others. A simple smile or hug is a good start.

Showing unconditional love to those around you sparks the flame and others want to follow you and be with you.

Leading by example may be a good start to show the love you want to receive. Speak kindly of others and show compassion. That shows you care.

*****

Dear God,

Thank you for loving me. Be with me as I show love to others in your kingdom. Amen.

AUGUST 23

> The secret things belong unto the Lord our God: but those things which are revealed belong unto us and to our children forever, that we may do all the words of this law. (Deuteronomy 29:29)

The secret things belong to God. The scripture mentions things revealed to you that belong to you.

God's word is revealed to you in the form of the Bible. It is yours to obey and follow his teachings.

Other belongings you have include food, shelter, and family. You should be thankful for God's graciousness in providing for his children on earth.

Everyone has belongings; how to take care of them, is important in God's eyes. If you have a home, then he wants you to maintain it. If you have a family, show them love and look after them. God's blessings.

*****

Dear God,

Thank you for letting me belong to you. Keep me in your protection until I reach my heavenly home. Amen.

AUGUST 24

> And the blood shall be to you for a token upon the houses where ye are: and when I see the blood, I will pass over you, and the plague shall not be upon you to destroy you, when I smite the land of Egypt. (Exodus 12:13)

This was God's life insurance for the Israelites. He was destroying all the gods of Egypt. Evil came upon the land, and God needed to show judgment to the people.

You have the reassurance of God's love as he gave you the Bible. He loves you, and He sent his son to take away your sins. You have the life insurance of going to heaven someday.

Just have faith in Jesus. He is there for you when you need him the most. God's blessings.

*****

Dear God,

Thank you for providing the life insurance of Jesus in my life. Grant me wisdom to continue doing your work while I am on this earth. Amen.

AUGUST 25

> Jesus answered and said unto her, If thou knewest the gift of God, and who it is that saith to thee, Give me to drink; thou wouldest have asked of him, and he would have given thee living water. (John 4:10)

You can have God's universal love because he sent his beloved Son to take away your sins.

Do not be afraid of the devil since God is there to protect you from harm and danger. You just need to believe in Him and share His gospel with others.

Have you shared the gospel with someone today? It's never too late to start. God has confidence in you and is there guiding you along the way.

Call a friend or family member and ask if you can say a prayer for them. It may be just the encouragement they needed on that day. Maybe they are experiencing some insecurity or have other concerns; just being a friend and praying with them for comfort is the Christian thing to do. God's blessings.

*****

Dear God,

Thank you for loving me every day. Be with me and guide me to do your will here on earth. Amen.

AUGUST 26

> Jesus answered and said unto her, Whosoever drinketh of this water shall thirst again: But whosoever drinketh of the water that I shall give him shall never thirst; but the water that I shall give him shall be in him a well of water springing up into everlasting life. (John 4:13–14)

This verse is your promise of everlasting life. God refers to it as the water of life. Your thirst will be satisfied with eternal life. What a tremendous gift from God.

Are you satisfied with your life? Do you want to improve your life? Maybe you are at the end of your rope and need someone to tug on it to get you back up where you belong.

Let God into your life. Start by reading the Bible or joining a Bible class at church. Your life will be enriched twofold if you have faith in God's word. Give it a try by starting today. God's blessings.

*****

Dear God,

Thank you for the satisfaction of eternal life for me. Guide me in the direction to follow you to my heavenly home. Amen.

AUGUST 27

> He that hath an ear, let him hear what the Spirit saith un-to the churches; To him that overcometh will I give to eat of the tree of life, which is in the midst of the paradise of God. (Revelation 2:7)

Overcoming fear may be a powerful task. You do not want fear (evil) to control you. Learning to deal with fear may be as simple as taking advantage of new opportunities. The fear of public speaking could be eased by talking in front of a mirror or talking to a small group of friends at a time. Small steps can lead to more advancement, and the more you do it, the easier it becomes.

Another example is the fear of attending an event and not knowing what to say to others. Go to the event with a friend and ask them to introduce you to their friends; then you have similar backgrounds to talk about.

God wants you to turn evil or fear into good. Try challenging yourself next time fear overcomes you and ask yourself, "What would Jesus do?" (WWJD).

*****

Dear God,

Thank you for taking the evil and fear out of my life. Be with me to overcome fear obstacles in my life. Amen.

AUGUST 28

> But ye shall receive power, after that the Holy Ghost is come upon you: and ye shall be witness unto me both in Jerusalem, and in all Judea, and in Samaria, and unto the uttermost part of the earth. (Acts 1:8)

What a tremendous honor to be blessed by the Holy Ghost to be a witness for Jesus. One can only imagine the gratitude the disciples were feeling.

Have you ever received an important task or responsibility in your life? You want to do your best whatever the circumstance. After the task is completed, everyone thanks you for a job well done.

God wants you to witness for him to others. It can be something as simple as saying, "God bless you." Or telling your family you love them.

Life is too short. Be the best witness for Christ that you can be. Maybe someday you might be just that person who a stranger needed to brighten their day. God's blessings.

*****

Dear God,

Thank you for appointing me as your witness for Christ. Strengthen me to do your will until I see you in heaven. Amen.

AUGUST 29

> I have glorified thee on the earth: I have finished the work which thou gavest me to do. (John 17:4)

This verse talks about "finishing life's task" as it relates to eternal life. As John also mentions in John 3:15, "That whosoever believeth in him should not perish but have eternal life."

What a wonderful feeling knowing you have eternal life by believing. Give God the glory, knowing what he has done for you as a sinner. He continues to bless you no matter how many times you have disobeyed and fallen short of the glory of God.

Why not start today to glorify God. You may have been lax in the past, but today is as good as any to turn your life around and turn your heart to Jesus for redemption. He will protect you and guide you on the path to righteousness for his name's sake. God's blessings.

*****

Dear God,

Thank you for creating the earth and all its beauty. Be with me as I share your love with others. Amen.

AUGUST 30

> Finally, brethren, whatsoever things are true, whatsoever things are honest, whatsoever things are just, whatsoever things are pure, whatsoever things are lovely, whatsoever things are of good report; if there be any virtue, and if there be any praise, think on these things. (Philippians 4:8)

Based on this passage, here are some thoughts to consider:

- Truthfulness—speak the truth, put away lying, walk in peace
- Honesty—having a perfect balance in life, owe no man any-thing but love one another
- Purity—clean hands, a pure heart and obey the truth
- Meditation—meditate day and night to observe all that is written and have good success

What are your thoughts? Do any of these thoughts apply to you? If not, today is a good day to start having good thoughts about God.

Ask God to make you more pure and loving. God is there for you whenever you need him. Open your heart today and welcome him in with open arms. God's blessings.

*****

Dear God,

Thank you for providing me the "thoughts" to consider in my life. Be with me to start being more "pure" in your sight each day. Amen.

AUGUST 31

> For that ye ought to say, If the Lord will, we
> shall live, and do this, or that. (James 4:15)

This verse talks about planning and God's will. If you do God's will, it is the same as you would do to your brother or sister. Treating everyone with respect should be your everyday life goal.

Submission also relates to this verse which is the authority of the church. Yield yourself unto God and be instruments of his righteousness.

Do you follow God's will every day? You can try, but Satan tempts you and sometimes you fall short. That is part of life and God is aware of your shortcomings. He forgives your sins and welcomes you back to be His child.

Start today by giving your life to the Lord. Open your heart and welcome hope and joy and peace into your life.

*****

Dear God,

Thank you for providing your will for me to follow to enter eternal life. Be with me and grant me peace to allow you into my heart. Amen.

SEPTEMBER 1

> Have mercy upon me, O God, according to thy loving kindness: according unto the multitude of thy tender mercies blot out my transgressions. Wash me thoroughly from mine iniquity and cleanse me from my sin. (Psalm 51:1–2)

This is a good Psalm to begin a prayer with. The passage talks about forgiveness (blotting out) and cleansing (or cleaning) of your sins. God shows his mercy when he forgives you for any sins you have committed. He cleanses (washes) your iniquities away.

God's loving kindness shown to his people brings out his divine nature. He loves his people and wants the best for them.

The next time you are feeling alone, talk to God in prayer. Ask for forgiveness and cleansing and to be made new in your soul. He is ready to listen to your prayer and grant you his mercy.

*****

Dear God,

Thank you for showing me your mercy. Be with me to continue on your path of righteousness. Amen.

SEPTEMBER 2

> Serve the Lord with gladness: come before
> his presence with singing. (Psalm 100:2)

Gladness relates to joy and rejoicing. You can also serve your Lord in ways you may never have thought possible. Some people volunteer when they retire as it opens up a new realm of opportunities to serve and show gladness to others.

You may meet a friend who you may never have crossed paths with before and then in conversation realize you have a lot of common interests with them.

The Spirit will move you to give of yourself while showing kindness to others. Welcome the opportunity when it presents itself. God does work in mysterious ways to bring out your inner self and produce joy in your heart.

*****

Dear God,

Thank you for giving me joy in my heart. Give me the strength to move mountains one day at a time by witnessing to everyone around me. Amen.

SEPTEMBER 3

> Yea doubtless, and I count all things but loss for the excellency of the knowledge of Christ Jesus my Lord: for whom I have suffered the loss of all things, and do count them but dung, that I may win Christ. (Philippians 3:8)

This passage talks about consecration. Giving yourself to the ministry of the word through prayer. Having the knowledge of Christ and how he suffered and died for you. His sacrifice was great. Now it is up to you to show his abundant love to others around you.

The passage also relates to leaving parents and friends and following Jesus.

Could you leave all behind and follow Jesus? It is a tremendous commitment to give up things you are comfortable with and go on a path of unfamiliar territory.

You could also relate this change to a person entering the military, leaving behind the comfort of home, and traveling to a foreign environment. Sometimes it could be months or years before seeing family again. And sometimes the person returns as a different person, good or bad. Something to consider before making a big commitment.

*****

Dear God,

Thank you for consecrating me with your love. Give me the strength to follow your path to eternal life. Amen.

SEPTEMBER 4

> And behold, the angel of the Lord came upon him, and a light shined in the prison: and he smote Peter on the side, and raised him up, saying, Arise up quickly. And his chains fell off from his hands. (Acts 12:7)

This verse speaks about Peter's deliverance in answer to prayer. What a sight to behold, the light appearing in the prison and then the chains falling off from his hands.

This just proves how mighty our Redeemer is! He is all-knowing and all powerful!

Just when you think life couldn't get any worse, then a miracle happens, and you are granted redemption and a new outlook on life.

Has anything similar ever happened to you in life? You experienced an uneasy situation and wondered how you would get out of it, and then someone comes along and makes your life better by helping resolve the situation.

When a situation like this happens to you, thank God for rescuing you and giving you a second chance on life. You will be glad you did.

*****

Dear God,

Thank you for delivering Jesus into my life. Guide me to follow your direction so I stay on the path to righteousness for your name's sake. Amen.

SEPTEMBER 5

> Then Jesus said unto them, Verily, verily, I say unto you, Moses gave you not that bread from heaven; but my Father giveth you the true bread from heaven. For the bread of God is he which cometh down from heaven, and giveth life unto the world. (John 6:32–33)

This passage talks about the bread of life. If you eat this bread, you will live forever. Or if you believe in Him, you will also live forever. This passage also relates to heaven since God knows all things.

You may be faced with a difficult situation in life and not sure how to handle it, and you may make the wrong decision, with uneasy consequences to follow.

Asking God for assistance is always a better choice to make. Your decision may not have been a wise one. Taking your concern to God is the right way to go.

*****

Dear God,

Thank you for being my bread of life. Be with me to spread Your Word among the lost and erring until I reach eternal life. Amen.

SEPTEMBER 6

>For every man shall bear his own burden.
>(Galatians 6:5)

This passage speaks about every person taking responsibility for their own actions.

If you commit a crime or wrongdoing, you ultimately will be held responsible for the punishment. Sometimes the punishment is severe or jail time. People who commit crimes sometimes don't think of the consequences before they commit the crime.

God wants you to obey the laws or rules that are made by officials. One may think they can get away with a small wrong. God is watching you and so may be others. There are cameras watching you in a business setting, so eyes are everywhere when you least expect it.

Obeying the law is a Christian response to being responsible for your actions. It's a good thing to teach your children the right way of doing things also.

*****

Dear God,

Thank you for giving me a life of gratitude. Be with me as I share your undying love with others in your kingdom. Amen.

SEPTEMBER 7

> So built we the wall; and all the wall was joined together unto the half thereof: for the people had a mind to work. (Nehemiah 4:6)

This verse talks about builders. Builders carry their burdens together and ultimately building a project together to get a final outcome. God builds you up during your life to prepare you for life's adventures, challenges, and triumphs.

Whatever stage you are in life right now, it could make you happy right now knowing you have accomplished a triumph in life. Or it could make you sad if you are still living in your struggle and trying to figure out how to get through the challenge.

Starting today, take charge of your life. Put God as number one in your life. What a difference it will make having God as the driver in your life. Your life will be more focused. A daily prayer with God or devotion is a good start.

*****

Dear God,

Thank you for carrying the burden in my life. Be with me to guide me to your path of righteousness. Amen.

SEPTEMBER 8

> Or ministry, let us wait on our ministering: or he that teacheth, on teaching; or he that exhorteth, on exhortation: he that giveth, let him do it with simplicity; he that ruleth, with diligence; he that sheweth mercy, with cheer-fulness. (Romans 12:7–8)

These verses speak about various duties of the church ministry. Whether it be teaching, ministering, showing mercy, or being cheerful, all are important duties in God's eyes in spreading his Gospel to others.

If you were a church worker, what would be your strengths? Everyone is unique in God's eyes. Some people are leaders while others are better at being a church worker or behind-the-scenes person.

It doesn't matter in what capacity you serve in the church. Every task is important in showing love to others.

Find your strongpoint and give it a try. The church always welcomes volunteers who want to spread God's word. God's blessings.

*****

Dear God,

Thank you for giving me the opportunity to serve you in the church. Be with me and guide me to continue serving you in Your kingdom. Amen.

SEPTEMBER 9

> Dearly beloved, avenge not yourselves, but rather give place unto wrath: for it is written, Vengeance is mine; I will repay, saith the Lord. Therefore if thine enemy hunger, feed him; if he thirst, give him drink: for in so doing thou shalt heap coals of fire on his head. (Romans 12:19–20)

This passage talks about the Christian spirit. How you should treat others is the same way you would like to be treated. If someone you know is hungry, give them some food; likewise if there is someone who is thirsty, give them something to drink.

You may think about the Christian spirit, but do you show the spirit to others if the circumstance arises?

Starting today, show the Christian spirit to those around you. God loves a cheerful giver. Your life will be so much fuller once you start showing God's love to others.

*****

Dear God,

Thank you for showing me how to show the Christian spirit. Guide me to continue showing love to others in this world. Amen.

SEPTEMBER 10

> Let every soul be subject unto the higher powers. For there is no power but of God: the powers that be are ordained of God. Whosoever therefore resisteth the power, resisteth the ordinance of God: and they that resist shall receive to themselves damnation. (Romans 13:1–2)

These verses relate to the duties of the state. Every citizen has laws to abide by or ordinances to follow. In a big city, there may be more laws to follow than a smaller community. And there may be consequences if laws are not followed.

When you do not follow the rules, the devil is getting his way and may be tempting you. Do not let the devil rule, use your better judgment, and abide by the rules set forth.

Encourage others to follow rules and laws established by government or businesses around you. Rules are made and are meant to be followed.

*****

Dear God,

Thank you for providing me rules and ordinances to follow. Guide me to follow your rules for life. I look forward to meeting you in heaven someday. Amen.

SEPTEMBER 11

> Love worketh no ill to his neighbor: therefore love is the fulfilling of the law. (Romans 13:10)

Maybe you and your neighbor had a disagreement and neither one of you want to admit that you are wrong. Or maybe the circumstance was so bad that it created harm to you or your family.

Nevertheless, whatever the situation, try to resolve it with some sort of peaceful ending. Holding a grudge against someone is not the right thing to do.

God is ready to forgive you; now you must forgive those who have caused harm against you.

It is tough to do sometimes, but the sooner you let it go and move on, the better your life will become.

*****

Dear God,

Thank you for showing me how to love my neighbor. Sometimes it is difficult to do. Keep me in your grace and show mercy to me as I continue on this journey to eternal life. Amen.

SEPTEMBER 12

> For by grace are ye saved through faith; and that not of yourselves: it is the gift of God: Not of works, lest any man should boast. (Ephesians 2:8–9)

You alone are in control of your thoughts and actions. Focus on what you can control, and don't allow others to sway you in the wrong direction.

God has saved you by his grace; it is his gift to you. The Bible is His Word and guides you to his pathways.

Your life gets busy, and you get tempted by the devil to follow the wrong path. Stay focused on your faith to get you through difficult circumstances.

Focus on your thoughts through daily Bible reading, and your faith will be strengthened.

*****

Dear God,

Help me to stay focused on Your Word. Ward off any temptations by the devil. You alone are the stronghold of my life. Amen.

SEPTEMBER 13

> But without faith it is impossible to please him: for he that cometh to God must believe that he is, and that he is a rewarder of them that diligently seek him. (Hebrews 11:6)

God is the reward for them that seeketh Him. Do you ever wonder what your reward is after you do a good deed? It may not be a reward, it may simply be a thank you or a compliment for doing a good job.

Everyone likes to receive a compliment. It brings a smile to you, knowing someone notices something you did.

Try complimenting someone in your life and then take note of their response. Didn't that make you happy?

And so it is with God's love; it's contagious and you should want to share it with others. Open your heart and share it with those around you.

*****

Dear God,

Thank you for rewarding me with God's love. Continue to bless me so I can show love to others. Amen.

SEPTEMBER 14

> For ye had compassion of me in my bonds and took joyfully the spoiling of your goods, knowing in yourselves that ye have in heaven a better and an enduring substance. (Hebrews 10:34)

Rejoicing that your sins are forgiven is the salvation promised to God's people.

God wants you to endure and look to him when life gets tough and unpredictable. He is always there for you when you need him the most.

Put God in your life today. Give him a chance to show you hope and grace.

Maybe it's been a struggle lately in your life. God understands everyone has challenges in this world. Open up your heart and let God give you peace.

*****

Dear God,

Thank you for showing compassion in my life. Grant me grace and wisdom to show others your love. Amen.

SEPTEMBER 15

> Not forsaking the assembling of ourselves together, as the manner of some is; but exhorting one another: and so much the more, as ye see the day approaching. (Hebrews 10:25)

This verse relates to church attendance. Where do you stand on the issue of church attendance? Some people go to church every Sunday. Some people only go on holidays when it is convenient for them. Others do live streaming to hear the church service on their phone or computer.

Whatever is your preferred method, it's good. God does want you to hear the Word and keep it.

Try putting an emphasis on hearing God's word more frequently. Once you feel comfortable hearing God's word, try sharing his word with others. Invite someone to Bible class or to attend church with you. You will be surprised how easy it may become after you try it a few times. God's blessings.

*****

Dear God,

Thank you for allowing me to attend church to hear your word. Be with me on my journey to show your love to others. Amen.

SEPTEMBER 16

> For in many things we offend all. If any man offend not in word, the same is a perfect man, and able also to bridle the whole body.
> (James 3:2)

God wants you to take control of your language. No one is perfect, it's human nature. You try to say the right thing, but sometimes the way it comes out it may offend someone.

God understands the human imperfections people reveal. As the saying goes, "Think before you speak," may just apply in this instance.

If you are angry, it's a good idea to calm down before words are said that could hurt a person's feelings. God wants you to build a person up and say good things about them. Showing kindness to one another is the better way to react to a conflicting situation.

Jesus loves a cheerful giver. Try giving a compliment the next time temptation comes upon you.

*****

Dear God,

Thank you for allowing me to control my language. It's a difficult task to do. Grant me grace to show love and kindness to others around me. Amen.

SEPTEMBER 17

> Then said Jonathan unto David, Whatsoever thy soul desireth, I will even do it for thee. (1 Samuel 20:4)

This passage talks about friendship. Another passage in the Bible also relates to friendship, John 15:13, "Greater love hath no man than this, that a man lay down his life for his friends."

What is friendship? When you would do just about anything for someone you care about. It could be a small favor for someone. Or an errand for someone homebound. Or even going above and beyond and giving of your time to make that person feel special.

A true friend is someone who cares for someone else and wants the best for them. As you go through life, you will encounter many friends. Some will come and go, and some may be your friends for your entire lifetime.

Cherish your friendships you have made over the years. Those friends hold you very dear and value your special time together.

*****

Dear God,

Thank you for friendship. Be with me to hold my friends near and dear to me as they are a gift from you. Amen.

SEPTEMBER 18

> I am the true vine, and my Father is the husbandman. Every branch in me that beareth not fruit, he taketh away: and every branch that beareth fruit, he purgeth it, that it may bring forth more fruit. (John 15:1–2)

Christ is the true vine that beareth fruit. Pruning a tree is necessary to bring forth abundant fruit in the future.

God wants you to constantly be thinking about the fruit of the spirit. How can you share God's word with others around you? You could be a minister, a teacher, or a church worker. Those are just a few individuals involved with a church or school.

God encourages other individuals to also share his word. Parents can teach their children about God. There are weekend retreats or conferences which involve large groups of people. Or you may consider inviting a family to join you on a Sunday morning for church.

*****

Dear God,

Thank you for being my true vine and keeping me connected to your tree of life. Be with me to follow your path to eternal life. Amen.

SEPTEMBER 19

> Commit thy way unto the Lord; trust also
> in him; and he shall bring it to pass. (Psalm 37:5)

Commitment is a powerful word. Your commitment to your family, your job, or your friends is a daily task. Being committed to God means reading the Bible daily and living His Word through your actions.

Trust also in God for direction that he provides you. Trust involves the little things in life, not just the big ones. Maybe attending a Bible study at church, and then volunteering to lead the event in the future.

God uses you in ways you would never have imagined. Trust his guidance and miracles will happen. Your eyes will be opened to many creative opportunities in the future.

*****

Dear God,

Thank you for your guidance in my life. Please provide me with the trust to live my life in accordance with your will. Amen.

SEPTEMBER 20

> And in that day ye shall ask me nothing. Verily, verily, I say unto you, Whatsoever ye shall ask the Father in my name, he will give it to you. (John 16:23)

Prayer is a source for joy. God wants you to bring your re-quests to him in prayer. Since God is all-powerful, he can grant prayer requests to you. It may not be the answer you are looking for, but God will give you a response the best way he sees fit for you.

Prayer is very powerful. Do you talk to God every day in prayer? If not, today would be a good time to start. Taking your concerns to God in prayer will enrich your life tremendously.

A talk with God may be just what you need when life gets tough or your days are troubled. Seek patience and kindness from God. Ask God for guidance for a life full of joy.

*****

Dear God,

Thank you for putting joy in my life. Be with me to follow your path of righteousness to my eternal home. Amen.

SEPTEMBER 21

> And God hath set some in the church, first apostles, secondarily prophets, thirdly teachers, after that miracles, then gifts of healings, helps, governments, diversities of tongues. Are all apostles? Are all prophets? Are all teachers? Are all workers of miracles? Have all the gifts of healing? Do all speak with tongues? Do all interpret? (1 Corinthians 12:28–30)

The passage speaks about the gifts of the Holy Spirit. Everyone has unique gifts or talents.

What are your unique gifts God has given you?

- Are you a medical person?
- Do you excel in speaking?
- Are you a person who helps people (maybe a miracle worker)?

Everyone has their own talents. It doesn't matter how great or small you think your talent is. God knows you are special in his eyes. He wants you to help others in whatever capacity you are able to help. He loves a cheerful giver.

*****

Dear God,

Thank you for giving me the many gifts you have to offer. Guide me to follow your direction to share your love and gifts with others. Amen.

SEPTEMBER 22

> And after these things I heard a great voice of much people in heaven, saying, Alleluia; Salvation, and glory, and honor, and power, unto the Lord our God. (Revelation 19:1)

This verse relates to the Hallelujah Chorus in heaven. Some of the chorus includes:

- Heavenly Praise—multitude of angels praising God
- Glorifying God—giving glory, honor, and power to God
- Salvation of God—God is your strength and the mighty one
- God's Glory—filled with the Holy Ghost
- God's Power—he is strong; divided the sea with his power; setteth the mountains with his strength

Do you know just how powerful God is? You may compare him to Hercules or Superman, but not so; he is all-powerful and all-knowing.

*****

Dear God,

Thank you for sending the chorus of heaven into my life. Keep me in your care to handle difficult situations. Amen.

SEPTEMBER 23

> Greater love hath no man than this, that a
> man lay down his life for his friends. (John 15:13)

Christ's love comes in many forms. Some of the characteristics of Christ's love include:

- Unchangeable
- Divine
- Self-sacrificing
- Inseparable
- Manifested by his death

And the best characteristic is friendship. What sacrifice would you make for your friends? Would you lay down your life for your friends? That's a tough call!

You hear people donating a kidney to a loved one or a stranger. That alone is a tough decision to make. One would need to get tested to make sure they are compatible. But, oh, what a miracle it would be if you were the recipient of that organ donation.

This is a perfect example of laying down your life for someone. Won't you consider an organ donation if you are asked.

*****

Dear God,

Thank you for laying down your life for me. Grant me patience to go out and witness to others. Amen.

SEPTEMBER 24

> Now faith is the substance of things hoped for, the evidence of things not seen. (Hebrews 11:1)

This passage speaks of faith as the assurance of things hoped for and proving of things not seen.

As it relates to your faith, you have faith in Jesus as your Savior, even though you cannot see him. So true is God's love for you that you may not see it, but it is there every day.

You need to believe and have hope in God. He is there for you, listening to your every spoken word. He watches over you and protects you from harm.

Let God into your life today. You will be blessed in your faith and in your life. A simple prayer to God every morning or a short devotion is a good starting point. God's blessings.

*****

Dear God,

Thank you for giving me the faith of a child to come to you with my supplications. Keep me in your loving arms so I can follow your path to eternal life. Amen.

SEPTEMBER 25

> Keep yourselves in the love of God, looking for the mercy of our Lord Jesus Christ unto eternal life. (Jude 1:21)

Do you know what heaven will be like? No one does. You can only imagine it will be beyond your wildest dreams. It will be the most beautiful place you have ever seen. It will be filled with pure happiness. You will be able to see Jesus in his royal splendor. What a sight to behold!

Just knowing God has a place reserved for you in heaven someday is very special. This home on earth is just a temporary one, and your real home awaits you in heaven.

What a blessing to know that you have eternal life because you are a Christian. The joy of knowing Jesus and what he did for you on the cross is a comforting thought. Praise be to God.

*****

Dear God,

Thank you for granting me eternal life. Be with me and grant me your peace to share your love with others in this world. Amen.

SEPTEMBER 26

> If I then, your Lord and Master, have washed your feet; ye also ought to wash one another's feet. (John 13:14)

This is a great example of humility. Jesus washing the disciples' feet. He shows his humble service as an example that you should show humility to others.

Do you show humility to others around you? Showing compassion to mankind is a great example of how God wants Christians to be.

God wants you to be doers of his word and not hearers only.

God has chosen you to be a child of God. He wants you to go out into the world and share his love with others.

Focus on living a life serving God with a humble heart. What better time to start than today.

*****

Dear God,

Thank you for putting humility in my life. Grant me wisdom and patience to follow your example to share your love with others. Amen.

SEPTEMBER 27

> Therefore with joy shall ye draw water out
> of the wells of salvation. (Isaiah 12:3)

Joy is promised to believers, and thirst is satisfied.

How many times have you been really thirsty and longed for a drink of water? Then when you drank the water, you were satisfied. So it is with God's Word; he wants you to long to hear and learn the Bible. As in the water, he wants you to be satisfied after thirsting for his Gospel.

It's not just hearing the word, but also living your life as a Christian. Living a life of service to God. Sharing his word with others.

Try starting a life with God as your focal point. Today is as good as any to dedicate your life to serving God and opening your heart to sharing his love. God's blessings.

*****

Dear God,

Thank you for putting joy and salvation into my heart. Be with me and protect me from the evil ones. Grant me grace to follow you on my path to eternal life. Amen.

SEPTEMBER 28

> When the Son of man shall come in his glory, and all the holy angels with him, then shall he sit upon the throne of his glory. (Matthew 25:31)

This passage refers to judgment and sitting on God's right hand. Some other characteristics of Christ's glory include:

- Manifest
- Shared
- Beheld
- Revealed

Christ's glory is magnificent. Oh, to behold his glory! Some people wait a lifetime to be able to experience glory in their lives. In the Bible, God makes it known to his people that glory is for everyone.

*****

Dear God,

Thank you for sharing your glory with me and others around me. Help me to focus on your saving grace. Amen.

SEPTEMBER 29

> How then shall they call on him in whom they have not believed? And how shall they believe in him of whom they have not heard? And how shall they hear without a preacher? And how shall they preach, except they be sent? As it is written, How beautiful are the feet of them that preach the gospel of peace and bring glad tidings of good things! (Romans 10:14–15)

Go and preach the gospel to all people as God refers to missions in this scripture. He wants you to be a messenger and tell others of the good tidings and great joy of Jesus.

How can you be a messenger for Jesus? You can start by opening up your Bible and finding the various passages referring to God's love, hope, and salvation for all mankind.

Starting a daily devotion also provides a good inspiration to be more into God's word. And prayer ties all of this together. God's blessings.

*****

Dear God,

Thank you for teaching me to be a missionary in Your kingdom. Grant me grace to follow your example to share your love with others. Amen.

SEPTEMBER 30

> For this is the covenant that I will make with the house of Israel after those days, saith the Lord; I will put my laws into their mind and write them in their hearts: and I will be to them a God, and they shall be to me a people. (Hebrews 8:10–11)

This verse illustrates the New Covenant and the Seven Editions of Divine Law:

1. Written on nature (Psalm 19:1); God shows his handiwork.
2. Written on conscience (Romans 2:15); the conscience bearing witness.
3. Written on Tables of Stone (Exodus 24:12); commandments written on stone.
4. The entire scriptures (Romans 15:4); written for your learning.
5. Christ the illustrated edition (John 1:14); the Word of God.
6. Written on the heart (Hebrews 8:10); the New Covenant or Law.
7. The outward Christian life living epistles (2 Corinthians 3:2–3), believers, living epistles.

*****

Dear God,

Thank you for giving me your covenant. Guide me to follow your path to righteousness. Amen.

OCTOBER 1

> Remember now thy Creator in the days of thy youth, while the evil days come not, nor the years draw nigh, when thou shalt say, I have no pleasure in them. (Ecclesiastes 12:1)

God wants his people to remember what he created. It was truly a miracle that was created and how it was done. Every day was created uniquely with immense detail. At the end of each day, God commented with, "And God saw that it was good."

God had much thought as to how he wanted the earth to look and what he wanted each thing he created to represent.

Creation was marvelous until Adam and Eve sinned and fell short of his glory.

Everyone sins in this world. That is why Jesus died on the cross to take away your sin.

God wants you to rejoice at his creation. It was created with you in mind.

*****

Dear God,

Thank you for your creation. Grace me with your protection. Amen.

OCTOBER 2

> The steps of a good man are ordered by the
> Lord: and he delighteth in his way. (Psalm 37:23)

God directs your steps in life. He is there for you, making you stay on the path to righteousness. God numbers your steps just like he numbers the hairs on your head.

God watches your steps, so you don't stumble along your journey. Life has its ups and downs; it's knowing which path to go on. You have many decisions to make in life; choosing the right one is critical. If you make a bad decision, there could be consequences. People are faced with uncertainty sometimes in their life; having God on your side is always the right choice.

The next time you are faced with a difficult decision, say a prayer to God for guidance and protection. God is always willing to hear your prayer.

*****

Dear God,

Thank you for directing my steps in life. Protect me on my journey so I may witness to others in Your kingdom. Amen.

OCTOBER 3

> Again, the kingdom of heaven is like unto treasure hid in a field; that which when a man hath found, he hideth, and for joy thereof goeth and selleth all that he hath, and buyeth that field. (Matthew 13:44)

The hidden treasure is the kingdom of heaven. It is like a spirit hidden and then found or revealed.

That's how it is with God's love. It is there when we are ready for it. God gives you family and friends on this earth to enjoy. It's up to you to find the happiness and joy in your life and share it with others.

Once you find it, your life will be filled with God's eternal life. It's a great feeling to know salvation awaits you. God's blessing.

Find a meditation time that works for you. You will be surprised how your life will improve after you have your intimate conversations with God on a daily basis.

*****

Dear God,

Thank you for revealing the hidden treasure to me. Please keep me in your protection so I may see you in heaven someday. Amen.

OCTOBER 4

> Bless the Lord, O my soul: and all that is
> within me, bless his holy name. (Psalm 103:1)

This is the Thanksgiving prayer of praise. You should glorify God for the many blessings He gives you. Some of the many blessings God provides include water, rain for the crops to grow, and the food you eat.

You should thank God for the many blessings He bestows upon you. It would be difficult to imagine life without the basic needs to depend upon for your daily living.

You should thank God daily for all He has done for you in your life. Include in your daily prayer the appreciation of having an abundant and fruitful life. God's grace is contagious; he wants you to share His love and grace with others.

*****

Dear God,

Thank you for showing me how to praise your name. Be with me and protect me in your grace and mercy. Amen.

OCTOBER 5

> And I say unto you, Ask, and it shall be given you; seek, and ye shall find; knock, and it shall be opened unto you. For everyone that asketh receiveth; and he that seeketh findeth; and to him that knocketh it shall be opened. (Luke 11:9–10)

This is God's threefold promise: ask, seek, and knock. God wants you to ask Him for what you need. Then He wants you to seek or find what you requested of Him. And lastly, knock and the door of opportunity will be granted or opened for you.

One of God's gifts to you is opportunity. How often do you have the opportunity to do something great in life, for yourself or some-one else? You may think it's just luck, but God puts the opportunity there for you to enjoy.

So the next time you are presented with an unexpected opportunity, thank God for his unmeasurable mercy upon you. Enjoy the gift He gives you, especially if you can share it with someone else.

*****

Dear God,

Thank you for your threefold promise to me. I look forward to every opportunity you provide me as a gift from above. Amen.

OCTOBER 6

> For I was envious at the foolish, when I saw
> the prosperity of the wicked. (Psalm 73:3)

This verse speaks about prosperity. You may despise others or try to find their faults. God wants you to lift up others in His grace and wisdom.

Create good habits and do what is right while you are on this earth. Look for the good in others and help them prosper as well.

Promoting love and happiness throughout the world will make your life more enjoyable and worthwhile. A lot of time parents will pass along their favorite traits or sayings to their children. These are called memories. Life is all about making memories on your journey through life. God's blessings.

*****

Dear God,

Thank you for giving me prosperity while I am on this earth. Grant me the wisdom to show others the love you have shown to me. Amen.

OCTOBER 7

> And among the cities which ye shall give unto the Levites there shall be six cities for refuge, which ye shall appoint for the manslayer, that he may flee thither: and to them ye shall add forty and two cities. (Numbers 35:6)

This passage refers to the refuge the Levites received as their inheritance, or their surrounding communities.

If you live in a big city there may be suburbs which surround you. It may be comforting to go outside the city to a more relaxing area in the suburbs. Everyone prefers a different lifestyle. Or maybe you enjoy living further out into the country and the laid-back lifestyle.

Just simply enjoy the life you have and follow the path God has provided for you. Every day could be an adventure.

*****

Dear God,

Thank you for being my refuge when I needed you the most. Be with me and protect me through life as my journey continues down the path of righteousness. Amen.

OCTOBER 8

> Peace I leave with you, my peace I give unto you: not as the world giveth, give I unto you. Let not your heart be troubled, neither let it be afraid. (John 14:27)

This passage talks about the legacy of peace. It provides strength and blessings to all believers. Even though there is trouble and tribulation in the world, God wants you to be of good cheer as he alone rules the world.

Also, relating to this passage, are the seven gifts of Christ:

1. Rest—everyone needs rest in their life
2. Keys of the kingdom—power to forgive sins
3. Power over evil spirits—no evil shall harm you
4. Living water—as you drink the water, you will never thirst
5. Bread of heaven—if you eat of the bread, you will live forever
6. Eternal life—you shall never perish
7. Legacy of peace—strength and blessing

*****

Dear God,

Thank you for providing me strength in my life. Give me courage to follow your path to eternal life. Amen.

OCTOBER 9

> Jesus answered, Verily, verily, I say unto thee, Except a man be born of water and of the Spirit, he cannot enter into the kingdom of God. (John 3:5)

This verse talks about regeneration or spiritual vision obtained by the word of God or faith. It's a beautiful vision being sanctified by salvation and full of faith.

Baptism is also referred to in this verse, as born of the water, and baptism can now save you.

The spiritual kingdom is within you if you just believe. God wants believers in his kingdom to help do the work of calling the lost into his flock.

Regeneration takes on various forms and you may relate to one of them.

- Birth of a New Spirit —— Ezekiel 36:26
- Essential to Spiritual Vision —— John 3:3
- Necessary to Salvation —— Titus 3:5
- Obtained by Faith —— 1 John 5:1

*****

Dear God,

Following in God's footsteps may be a tall order for me to fill, but having faith will allow me to continue on my journey to eternal life. God, grant me peace. Amen.

OCTOBER 10

> Let us therefore fear, lest, a promise being
> left us of entering into his rest, any of you should
> seem to come short of it. (Hebrews 4:1)

This verse refers to entering rest by faith. You may experience godly fear, spiritual rest, or spiritual loss.

Whatever state you are in, keep your faith in God and look to the heavens for inspiration.

Everyone needs rest. After you have had a long day at work or working on a project, rest is essential to relax your weary bones or muscles. There may even be some pain in your muscles that may require some medical intervention.

That may be one reason God made the Sabbath day—to give everyone a day of rest. Some people may need a day of rest every week, and others may not need so much rest. Whatever your situation, listen to your body; if you are tired, take time to care for yourself and get some needed rest. God's blessings.

*****

Dear God,

Thank you for giving me a day of rest. The rest provides relaxation when it is needed the most. Be with me to continue on your path to eternal life. Amen.

OCTOBER 11

> But now is Christ risen from the dead and become the first fruits of them that slept. (1 Corinthians 15:20)

This passage talks about the certainty of Christ's resurrection. First fruits refers to having new life through the Word of God.

What a wonderful feeling knowing Jesus ascended into heaven and conquered death and sin for all believers.

God's grace and mercy are all around you. Keep your heart open for glorifying God.

Include those in need in your daily prayers, asking for comfort and compassion where needed. Share your love and kindness also to those in need.

You may just need that same comfort for yourself someday.

*****

Dear God,

Thank you for your resurrection for me. Guide me to follow your path to righteousness so I can be with you in heaven someday. Amen.

OCTOBER 12

> There shall no evil befall thee, neither shall
> any plague come nigh thy dwelling. (Psalm 91:10)

Safety is talked about in this verse. You should be fearless among your enemies.

God wants you to be aware of your surroundings and always look out for your safety. You may be in a crowd, especially at an event where there is a large group of people; be cautious of those around you.

Asking God for protection may be beneficial so harm doesn't befall you. Children look to their parents for protection when they are young because they may not know what harm could lie ahead of them.

If you are a parent, then you know how much a child looks up to you. Just like you should look up to your Father in heaven for security and protection.

*****

Dear God,

Thank you for safety in my life. Give me faith to follow down the path to eternal life until I reach heaven someday. Amen.

OCTOBER 13

> And the seventy returned again with joy, saying, Lord, even the devils are subject unto us through thy name. (Luke 10:17)

This verse talks about the joy in service. You can rejoice with great joy that you have eternal life through Christ.

The faithful serve the Lord with gladness and don't ask for anything in return.

How do you serve the Lord in your life? Are you active in the church or school? Are you involved in your community or with friends? Taking an interest in others is the Christian thing to do. Jesus loves a cheerful giver.

If you haven't committed to serving your Lord, today is a good time to start. Take one day at a time until you feel comfortable. In no time, serving the Lord will become a natural part of your life.

*****

Dear God,

Thank you for teaching me how to serve in your kingdom. Be with me and protect me so I can serve you more in the future. Amen.

OCTOBER 14

> Verily, verily, I say unto you, He that entereth not by the door into the sheepfold, but climbeth up some other way, the same is a thief and a robber. But he that entereth in by the door is the shepherd of the sheep. To him the porter openeth; and the sheep hear his voice: and he calleth his own sheep by name, and leadeth them out. And when he putteth forth his own sheep, he goeth before them, and the sheep follow him: for they know his voice. (John 10:1–4)

This relates to the shepherd; Christ is your shepherd. He leads you down the path of righteousness. He promises his followers He will guide you if you believe in Him.

How many times have you been led astray and not followed instructions when told? You may have been tempted by the devil to go down another path and things didn't go so well. You may have had to return to the beginning and start your journey over again.

*****

Dear God,

Thank you for being my shepherd when I strayed from your path. Protect me so I stay on the right path to righteousness for Your Name's sake. Amen.

OCTOBER 15

> O taste and see that the Lord is good: blessed
> is the man that trusteth in him. (Psalm 34:8)

The goodness of God is described in this passage. God does not judge sinners, he teaches sinners the way. He loves righteousness as his mercy endures for all people. God's mercy is from everlasting to everlasting and his truth reaches unto the clouds.

God makes salvation possible; through his mercy he saved us by the washing of regeneration and renewing of the Holy Spirit.

What a joy to experience God's mercy and compassion every day on this earth. Don't ever take life for granted; life is too short. Life could be going great for you today, and then evil comes into the picture with no notice. If there is someone you have been meaning to contact (a lost relative or friend), reach out to them today. Tomorrow may never happen. God's blessings.

*****

Dear God,

Thank you for showing me your goodness and mercy. Be with me and protect me from harm and danger. Amen.

OCTOBER 16

> But God hath revealed them unto us by his Spirit: for the Spirit searcheth all things, yea, the deep things of God. For what man knoweth the things of a man, save the spirit of man which is in Him? Even so the things of God knoweth no man, but the Spirit of God. (1 Corinthians 2:10–11)

The passage speaks about the Holy Spirit as a teacher. The Holy Spirit gives understanding and faith.

God wants you to have faith in the Holy Spirit and look to him as being the almighty one. He is your hope of glory.

God knows all things. He knows everything about you. Open your heart to the Spirit and speak your mind. Your prayer life will be enriched if you give God a chance to show mercy on you. God can do great things for your life. As you go down your life journey, give God the glory for all the graces he has showered upon you in your life.

*****

Dear God,

Thank you for sending the Spirit to be the teacher in my life. Grant me grace to follow your path to righteousness. Amen.

OCTOBER 17

> When thou sittest to eat with a ruler, consider diligently what is before thee: And put a knife to thy throat, if thou be a man given to appetite. (Proverbs 23:1–2)

This verse talks about temperance. It relates to having an appetite also.

When you study God's Word, you have an appetite to learn more. You long for studying what Jesus did for you and how you can be a better Christian.

Eating can be synonymous with hearing God's Word and then sharing it with others around you. You need food for your spirit, and you get that from Bible studies, going to church, and having a daily devotion.

Focus on having an appetite for God's Word. It takes time to be enriched in God's Word. Today is as good as any to start your walk with God.

*****

Dear God,

Thank you for giving me an appetite to learn God's Word. Grant me grace to share your love with others. Amen.

OCTOBER 18

> Bring ye all the tithes into the storehouse, that there may be meat in mine house, and prove me now herewith, saith the Lord of hosts, if I will not open you the windows of heaven, and pour you out a blessing, that there shall not be room enough to receive it. (Malachi 3:10)

This passage talks about the tithes to the Lord. Some people still tithe to the church, while others give generously. It doesn't matter what amount you give to the church, as long as you give from your heart.

God sends you blessings from above and has open arms for you to give an amount from your heart. Whatever the spirit moves you to give; and give as often as possible. This can be time, talent, and treasures.

Some people make donations to the church for a special occasion or in memory of a loved one. Your decision should be between you and God and with a thankful heart.

*****

Dear God,

Thank you for teaching me to tithe. Your grace and mercy has been so generous to me over the years. Grant me grace to continue giving to Your kingdom. Amen.

OCTOBER 19

> I, therefore, the prisoner of the Lord, beseech you that ye walk worthy of the vocation wherewith ye are called, With all lowliness and meekness, with longsuffering, forbearing one another in love; endeavoring to keep the unity of the Spirit in the bond of peace. There is one body, and one Spirit, even as ye are called in one hope of your calling. (Ephesians 4:1–4)

This passage speaks of Christian unity. And it continues to talk about humility, meekness, peace, longsuffering, and forbearance.

As you walk with the Spirit, your belief in God is unique. Only you can know how you feel and take it to the Lord in prayer.

God is there to hear your supplications and answer your prayers.

As a member of the body of Christ, you can take comfort knowing that Jesus died to take away your sins. Every day is a new start of your life. God's blessing.

*****

Dear God,

Thank you for your Christian unity in my life. Grant me peace to know and to do your will while on this earth. Amen.

OCTOBER 20

> I said in mine heart, Go to now, I will prove thee with mirth, therefore enjoy pleasure: and, behold, this also is vanity. Ecclesiastes 2:1

This passage relates to vanity or emptiness. God wants you to put away evil and instead rejoice in him.

Sometimes one might carry a grudge from a past incident and are too proud to apologize or let it go. God wants you to forgive and move on with your life.

A grudge can weigh you down and make you sad or uneasy at times.

God wants you to have the grace to forgive others and also asks you to apologize when you might have said or done something wrong against another person. A load will be lifted off your shoulders, and you will feel like a renewed child of God.

You can start today with your new life, and let God open your heart with gratitude and thanksgiving for his mercy he shows to you. His love for you is enduring.

*****

Dear God,

Thank you for helping me rid myself of evil and for learning to praise you more. Grant me patience to follow your path for a more righteous life. Amen.

OCTOBER 21

> Son of man, speak to the children of thy people, and say unto them, When I bring the sword upon a land, if the people of the land take a man of their coasts, and set him for their watchman: If when he seeth the sword come upon the land, he blow the trumpet, and warn the people; Then whosoever heareth the sound of the trumpet, and taketh not warning; if the sword come, and take him away, his blood shall be upon his own head. (Ezekiel 33:2–4)

This passage talks about a watchman. He warns the people ahead of time of danger.

Likewise, you should always be on guard of danger lurking around you. God wants you to be on guard when you might be in a dangerous situation. The devil is always tempting you to do something that is not pleasing to God.

Say a prayer for protection if you think you are in a dangerous or uncomfortable situation. God will watch over you and guide you in the direction he wants you to go.

The next time you have a thought about life, focus on your inner feelings and see if there are patterns from your past feelings and how you can change them.

*****

Dear God,

Thank you for being my watchman in my life. Grant me wisdom to be on guard when in a dangerous situation. Amen.

OCTOBER 22

> A fountain of gardens, a well of living waters, and streams from Lebanon. (Song of Solomon 4:15)

Living water is a gift of Christ to believers. God wants you to be satisfied in His Word, praising Him with your lips.

Listening to His Word and believing in his powerful message of salvation will lead you to this living water.

God will feed your hungry soul with goodness and mercy throughout your life. Take time to give God your heart and spirit. He is there with an open heart to hear your requests.

God will guide you through the turbulent waters of life. Be not afraid but look up to Him for protection and guidance. God's blessings.

*****

Dear God,

Thank you for providing me with your water of life so I may never thirst. You alone are my protector. Guide me to serve you while I am on this earth. Amen.

OCTOBER 23

> Happy is the man that findeth wisdom, and the man that getteth understanding. (Proverbs 3:13)

Everyone wants happiness, knowledge, and most of all, wisdom. Once you have obtained wisdom, you feel powerful and think you know all things.

Not so. God is the only one all-powerful. He provides you wisdom to go about your daily living. It is He who helps you endure all things and gives you eternal life.

He asks you to believe in Him. Believe that He is your prophet, priest, and king. He is there for you whenever you have need of him. Open up your heart and give Him praise through your voice and songs. Experience the joy of being with Him in everlasting life.

*****

Dear God,

Thank you for giving me your wisdom and understanding. Grant me your grace to give you praise on my journey to eternal life. Amen.

OCTOBER 24

> Notwithstanding the Lord stood with me, and strengthened me; that by me the preaching might be fully known, and that all the Gentiles might hear: and I was delivered out of the mouth of the lion. (2 Timothy 4:17)

This verse talks about evangelism. Knowing God's divine presence, His divine constancy, and His divine support is how God wants His gospel to be shared with others.

Evangelism may be the broad spectrum, but it entails all believers to preach His Word into all the world. He gives you strength to "roar like a lion" when sharing His Word with others.

Evangelism can be done by old as well as young people. No task is too small. Look around you. Is there someone you could show God's love to? Open your heart and give it a try. Sharing God's love with others may be easier than you think.

*****

Dear God,

Thank you for giving me the opportunity to evangelize to others. Be with me as I continue on my path to share your word with others. Amen.

OCTOBER 25

> I am the vine, ye are the branches. He that abideth in me, and I in him, the same bringeth forth much fruit: for without me ye can do nothing. (John 15:5)

In this passage, believers are described as the branches of the vine. You are helpless without God. Also, you are dependent on God; without Him you can do nothing.

When the passage speaks to "spiritual fruit," it refers to death of the old life, chastening, or pruning to bear more fruit, spiritual receptivity, or when you hear the Word and understand then bring forth more fruit.

How can you abide in Christ more in your life? Have you thought about pruning your actions and being more in tune with God's word?

You can start today with how you lead your life. You can be any age, young or old. God wants you as his child to dedicate your life to serving Him and showing love to others.

*****

Dear God,

Thank you for being the vine in my life. As a branch, it is up to me to bring others into Your kingdom. Guide me to lead by your example. Amen.

OCTOBER 26

> I will love thee, O Lord, my strength.
> (Psalm 18:1)

You have a God of love. Your family loves you very dearly. Love is what binds people together.

At every wedding ceremony, the minister preaches the sermon on love. It is a good reminder to couples that they made a pledge of love to each other at their own wedding, "Till death us do part." Some marriages last up to fifty to sixty years. That's a lot of love to share with each other!

How do you share love with others? Maybe it's your family to share love with. Or it could be close friends. Or maybe you share love with church members you see every Sunday. The important thing is that you are showing love to others as Jesus has shown his love to you. Even a small gesture to someone, by saying, "God loves you," is a special way of sharing God's love with others.

*****

Dear God,

Thank you for loving me as I am a sinner. Be with me and guide me to share your love with others. Amen.

OCTOBER 27

> And when his brethren saw that their father loved him more than all his brethren, they hated him, and could not speak peaceably unto him.
> Genesis 37:4

If you look hard enough, love exists everywhere. Do you have unconditional love for your family? God has unconditional love for you. Love abounds and can unlock doors for opportunity where you least expect it.

Love can be seen in your everyday life: at your job, at the store, in school, or with your family. Take time tomorrow to notice love in the air. It could be a person smiling at you or simply holding the door open for you. God is everywhere and will surprise you with these small gestures of love. Take note of them and thank God that his love abounds.

*****

Dear God,

Thank you for loving me. Be with me as I share your love with others in this world. Amen.

OCTOBER 28

> Jesus Christ the same yesterday, and today, and forever. (Hebrews 13:8)

God is unchangeable. He is eternal.

Revelation 22:13 refers to Christ as, "I am Alpha and Omega, the beginning and the end, the first and the last."

It is a great foundation of the world. Glorifying the Father for His beautiful creation of the world.

Have you thought about being part of Christ's foundation? It's not too late to become a believer and follow Him.

A simple daily devotion is a good start to your prayer life. Having a daily conversation with God will strengthen your well-being. God is your maker and encourages you to be your best self, starting today.

*****

Dear God,

Thank you for being unchangeable in my life. Be with me and protect me on my journey through life serving you. Amen.

OCTOBER 29

> Wherefore, my beloved brethren, let every man be swift to hear, slow to speak, slow to wrath; For the wrath of man worketh not the righteousness of God. (James 1:19–20)

Jesus is teaching you to listen more, restrain your tongue, hold the anger, and use more self-control.

God's righteousness is very powerful. He encourages you to be more hearers and doers of the Word.

Patience plays into this passage also. Focus on what would God want you to do for Him on this earth. Keep a log of your feelings for a week. Were they positive thoughts throughout the day? Did you get tempted by anger?

No one is perfect; try to be more patient and understanding of situations as they occur and see how your daily life can be enriched with more of God's love. God's blessings.

*****

Dear God,

Thank you for teaching me to listen more and control my tongue. Be with me to follow your path to righteousness to be with you in heaven. Amen.

OCTOBER 30

> Finally, be ye all of one mind, having compassion one of another, love as brethren, be pitiful, be courteous. (1 Peter 3:8)

This passage talks about showing compassion to others. Providing food or water to people, or even showing kindness to one another. Kindness can be shown in many forms such as: brotherly love, sympathy, or being courteous to those around you.

How do you show compassion or kindness to others? It can be a simple deed, as helping with errands or chores around the house. Your parents or those elderly in your community always appreciate an extra hand when it comes to tasks. They may not be as strong as they were in the past and struggle to do simple chores around the house anymore.

*****

Dear God,

Thank you for showing compassion upon me a sinful human being. Guard me as your child to show more kindness to others around me who need help. Amen.

OCTOBER 31

> Seeing ye have purified your souls in obeying the truth through the Spirit unto unfeigned love of the brethren, see that ye love one another with a pure heart fervently. (1 Peter 1:22)

This verse speaks of the power and performance of God's Word and shows obedience, love for the church, and brotherly love.

Love for the church also includes honor all men, love the brotherhood, fear God, and keep his commandments.

How do you love your church? What are some features you like about your church? Are there facets of your church you would like to change or see different?

Now is the time to offer any changes in your church. The first step would be to talk to your pastor. He has a willing ear and is open to suggestions. If you do talk to your pastor, you may be asked to volunteer your services to get programs started at your church; this is also referred to as "serving the Lord." God's blessings.

*****

Dear God,

Thank you for providing me with the power of Your Word. Grant me grace to share Your Word with others I meet in Your kingdom. Amen.

NOVEMBER 1

> For all this I considered in my heart even to declare all this, that the righteous, and the wise, and their works, are in the hand of God: no man knoweth either love or hatred by all that is before them. (Ecclesiastes 9:1)

God refers to the righteous; if you have ears, then let them hear. God wants you to be humble, and He will exalt you in time.

Be aware of evil; it can happen at any time. Know the difference between love and hatred, so you don't fall into the trap of the devil.

God wants you to be strong and stand on solid ground, despising the devil and his many tactics.

Jesus's love is all-powerful and will defend you from foolish ways. All you have to do is serve the Lord with gladness. Go out into the world and tell others what you have learned from Jesus your Savior.

*****

Dear God,

Thank you for letting me experience the good and bad things in this world. Be with me and keep me in your grace. Amen.

NOVEMBER 2

> And I gave my heart to seek and search out by wisdom concerning all things that are done under heaven: this sore travail hath God given to the sons of man to be exercised therewith. (Ecclesiastes 1:13)

This passage is about seeking wisdom; but you first need understanding of the Word of God. Every good gift comes from God. God wants you to enjoy life in Christ.

God also wants you to be aware of worldly cares. Do not be anxious of what to eat or what to drink, God is aware of your needs and will provide for you. You may also be around deceitful and unfruitful people. Please be aware of these and know there is good in this world. Look to God for direction and comfort.

Always seek God's wisdom if you are not sure which path to take when you are faced with challenging times.

*****

Dear God,

Thank you for providing me wisdom and understanding. Grant me grace to know and do your will while I am on this earth. Amen.

NOVEMBER 3

> The heavens declare the glory of God; and the firmament sheweth his handywork. (Psalm 19:1)

This verse talks about the creatures that shew God's glory. God's glory is in the heavens and in the clouds. What a marvelous sight to take in the glory from above.

Another majestic excellence to behold is God's works. Some of them include divine ways, divine justice, God of Truth, and songs of victory. God created nature with such magnitude and beauty.

If you take a drive around the state or country, you will see the beauty God has created. Instead of driving the freeways, take the backroads, and behold his beauty in mountains, in the streams and rivers, in the fields of crops, and in the animals grazing. God did create it all, and it is all unique to this world.

*****

Dear God,

Thank you for creating the world and showing me your glory and majestic excellence. You are truly marvelous in your works. Hold me in your grace that I may be all that you expect in a godly person. Amen.

NOVEMBER 4

> The lord is my shepherd; I shall not want. He maketh me to lie down in green pastures: he leadeth me beside the still waters. He restoreth my soul: he leadeth me in the paths of righteousness for his name's sake. (Psalm 23:1–3)

These verses speak of the Spirit providing rest, providing food, restoration, and leading you down the path to righteousness.

Christ is the shepherd, and you are the sheep. He leads you through life. Along the way, there are obstacles you encounter. Sometimes the decisions are difficult, and you may need to ask God in prayer what direction is the best to take. God is there for you every step of the way.

He provides guidance to you if you need it. He takes care of his people and all the creatures within.

Ask God for guidance and mercy when you are in a predicament and seek resolution.

*****

Dear God,

Thank you for providing me with green pastures. Grant me grace and wisdom to do your will while I am on this earth. Amen.

NOVEMBER 5

> Surely goodness and mercy shall follow me all the days of my life: and I will dwell in the house of the Lord forever. (Psalm 23:6)

This passage reflects on God's goodness, his mercy promised, and the love for His people.

Besides God's goodness, He does ask His people to keep His commandments and to trust in Him. God promises His mercy to all people. His people may need to repent of their sins, but He is just and will forgive their sins.

Give God a chance in your life today; open your heart and ask for forgiveness of your sins. He will reward you with grace and wisdom to go out into his world and share His love with others.

*****

Dear God,

Thank you for showing your goodness and mercy to me a lost and condemned servant. Show me your grace so I may follow your path to righteousness. Amen.

NOVEMBER 6

> O clap your hands, all ye people; shout unto God with the voice of triumph. For the Lord most high is terrible; he is a great King over all the earth. (Psalm 47:1–2)

These verses speak about the nations entertaining the kingdom of Christ. God's majesty and sovereignty are most high.

Do you sing loud praises to God every Sunday in church? God wants you to "Shout for Joy" in His house. That is the reason people join the choir at church, to shout with their voices. You may consider joining a church choir or a community choir if you would like to start singing. Or if you are not a good singer, consider taking lessons to learn a musical instrument. You are never too late to learn a new instrument. It may be as simple as learning to play the piano and even maybe try your hand at learning to play the violin. You might just surprise yourself at your hidden talent.

*****

Dear God,

Thank you for showing me your majesty on this earth. Show me your grace so I may serve you in Your kingdom. Amen.

NOVEMBER 7

> In whom we have redemption through his blood, the forgiveness of sins, according to the riches of his grace. (Ephesians 1:7)

This passage speaks about the riches of grace. God shows redemption to you through the blood of Jesus dying on the cross. His forgiveness is also shown by taking away your sins. You sin every day and fall short of the glory of God, but thanks be to God for his everlasting love for you.

God supplies you with whatever riches you need for your life. Accept the gifts as His grace and mercy.

You can glorify God by singing praises to Him. It can be done daily during your meditation with Him or weekly at the church you attend. It is important that you praise God for all He has done for you.

*****

Dear God,

Thank you for sharing the riches of God's grace with me. Be with me and grant me the grace to do your work while I am on this earth. Amen.

NOVEMBER 8

> Deliver me from mine enemies, O my God:
> defend me from them that rise up against me.
> (Psalm 59:1)

This verse speaks about divine defense. Defending God's people from the enemies.

Who do you go to when you are in a predicament and need someone to defend you? At school, you may go to a teacher or principal. At work, you may go to a supervisor or manager for assistance. In a family situation, you may go to your parents or someone else who is in authority. Whatever the circumstance, look for someone who can value your comments and will stand on your side. After the situation is resolved, thank God for being with you to find a workable solution.

And then learn from your mistakes or mishaps, so it doesn't happen again, or that you learn how to handle the situation in the future.

*****

Dear God,

Thank you for your divine defense for me against my enemies. Grant me grace to build up my confidence to face the enemies that may harm me. Amen.

NOVEMBER 9

> Truly my soul waiteth upon God: from him cometh my salvation. He only is my rock and my salvation; he is my defence; I shall not be greatly moved. (Psalm 62:1–2)

In these passages, you wait upon God, he is your rock and salvation. There is a stillness in the instruction. Stillness is essential. God asks that you stand still or wait, so as to let his word sink into your life.

In Psalm 46:10, it mentions to "Be still and know that I am God." He wants his people to realize what is happening in life and focus on the righteous acts of God.

Do you ever get anxious and don't want to wait for an event? Having patience is an important quality when a situation seems to last a long time. Even teaching children to learn patience can be a difficult task. Patience is an important virtue everyone can learn from.

*****

Dear God,

Thank you for being my rock and salvation in my life. Grant me peace to have the confidence to follow your path to everlasting righteousness. Amen

NOVEMBER 10

> And the light shineth in darkness; and the darkness com-prehended it not. (John 1:5)

Christ is the light of the world. When you walk in darkness, He is there beside you guiding you into untraveled territory.

You may think of Christ as your light in the world or as your flashlight so you can see your path ahead of you. So true, God shines in your heart and gives you the light or knowledge of His Word.

You can be enlightened by the Lord when there is darkness in your life. Look to God for His saving grace and abundant love when you feel overshadowed by darkness. He is there for you…just a prayer away. God's blessings.

*****

Dear God,

Thank you for being my light in the darkness of life. Be with me and show me your guiding light on my journey through life. Amen.

NOVEMBER 11

> For ye are bought with a price: therefore glorify God in your body, and in your spirit, which are God's. (1 Corinthians 6:20)

Wake up and be enlightened by God and his glory. Support your soul's growth. Enjoy every moment in every day; it is God's gift to you.

Your sins are forgiven, your slate is wiped clean; now go and tell others about Jesus. Small acts of kindness can show others your spirit.

Be interested in others' well-being and ask others how they know Jesus. If they don't know Jesus, invite them to church or a Bible study at your church. Support your local church by get-ting involved with the youth or elderly, who may need assistance. God's blessings.

*****

Dear God,

Thank you for paying the ultimate price for my salvation. Be with me as I support your ministry in the church and community. Amen.

NOVEMBER 12

> O come, let us sing unto the Lord: let us make a joyful noise to the rock of our salvation. Let us come before his presence with thanksgiving and make a joyful noise unto him with psalms. (Psalm 95:1–2)

God is referred to as a rock in this passage. He wants his people to praise Him, sing songs to Him, and make a joyful noise to him.

This passage sounds more like an Easter reflection. On Easter morning, you go to sunrise service and sing with loud voices praises to God and make a joyful noise. What joy it would be if every Sunday was Easter and churches were full of people. The pastors and organists would shout for joy.

How do you spend Easter with your family? Is it a family get-together? Do you host the dinner, or are you one who travels to be with your family?

Whatever the response, family is important, and you should spend time with the ones you love.

Make it a point today to spend time with a loved one whom you haven't seen in a while. You will be glad you did. God's blessings.

*****

Dear God,

Thank you for being the rock of my salvation. Teach me to sing praises to you every day. Amen.

NOVEMBER 13

> For the Lord is a great God, and a great King above all gods. In his hand are the deep places of the earth: the strength of the hills is his also. (Psalm 95:3–4)

God is showing you his greatness, that he is your king. He is all-powerful. He knows all things. He created all things. When you think of God, you think of Him like "Your majesty."

In various countries, there are rulers known as kings and queens. But God is truly your ruler and king of all the earth. You worship Him as the true God from above.

How do you honor your king? What special traits do you have to honor him? Starting your prayer journal today could be a great start. Keep a log each day, and when you look back, you will notice your prayer life has been enriched only twofold. God's blessings.

*****

Dear God,

Thank you for being my great God and great king. You alone are my strength. Be with me and grant me grace to know and do your will. Amen.

NOVEMBER 14

> The sea is his, and he made it: and his hands formed the dry land. O come, let us worship and bow down: let us kneel before the Lord our maker. (Psalm 95:5–6)

These verses talk about divine ownership by your creator. You should worship Your God. One of the positions of prayer is kneeling.

Kneeling is an older form of prayer. Some churches may still use the kneelers. It was a form of reverence in the church.

Worship can happen in many forms. Whatever position you feel comfortable with for your worship is acceptable. God just requests that you thank Him and praise Him for the creation he has made for you.

Give God the glory in any way you choose. God's blessings.

*****

Dear God,

Thank you for your creation and giving me the opportunity to worship with you. Give me the strength to show love to others on my journey to eternal life. Amen.

NOVEMBER 15

> For he is our God; and we are the people of his pasture, and the sheep of his hand. Today if ye will hear his voice, Harden not your heart, as in the provocation, and as in the day of temptation in the wilderness: When your fathers tempted me, proved me, and saw my work. (Psalm 95:7–9)

These verses speak about God's people and God's sheep. You are both. When you sin and fall short of God's glory, God forgives your sin and makes you whole again. You may compare this example to the shepherd, when the sheep are lost in the pasture. The shepherd knows his sheep and goes after the lost one to bring it back to the flock.

God, in turn, brings you back to His Word if you waiver. He is a loving God.

You may think if you do wrong in God's eyes, He will not accept you back into His kingdom. Not so. He welcomes you back with open arms to give you his grace.

*****

Dear God,

Thank you for making me one of your sheep and never letting me go astray. You alone are the Good Shepherd of my life. Be with me and protect me from harm and danger. Amen.

NOVEMBER 16

> Wait on the Lord: be of good courage, and he shall strengthen thine heart: wait, I say, on the Lord. (Psalm 27:14)

This passage talks about courage. Having the strength to go forward in life when faced with challenges and adversity.

As Deuteronomy 31:6 states, "He will not fail thee, nor forsake thee." Jesus is always with you no matter what the situation in life.

Do you ever find yourself in a situation where you need to exert extra courage to handle it? Sometimes the strength comes from above, and just a simple request to God makes all the difference in the world.

God hears your prayers and supplications. Ask for His guidance to carry on with your daily affairs.

*****

Dear God,

Thank you for providing me strength and courage to carry on my daily life. Watch over me and protect me from life's adversities that may arise. Amen.

NOVEMBER 17

> Where wast thou when I laid the foundations of the earth? declare, if thou hast understanding. Who hath laid the measures thereof, if thou knowest? Or who hath stretched the line upon it? Whereupon are the foundations thereof fastened? Or who laid the corner stone thereof; When the morning stars sang together, and all the sons of God shout-ed for joy? (Job 38:4–7)

This passage speaks about a foundation which relates to creation. And the stars in the sky sang together, what joy to hear the sound.

Have you laid the foundation of God in your life? Are you committed to serving your Lord?

Today is a great time to start serving in God's kingdom. Any task is worthwhile in the eyes of God. God's blessings.

*****

Dear God,

Thank you for creating the foundation for my life. Be with me to carry out your task of serving you in Your kingdom. Amen.

NOVEMBER 18

> He beholdeth all high things: he is a king
> over all the children of pride. (Job 41:34)

God makes known that He is all-powerful and king over all the earth. He is made without fear. He rules over all the sea with his majesty.

Are you ever afraid of what will happen tomorrow? Maybe you need to attend a big event and are not looking forward to at-tending. Could you be feeling anxiety? Or you may be uneasy of who might be there, and it may be an uncomfortable situation.

Say a silent prayer before you attend the event, asking God to be with you and protect you from any harm.

God does hear your prayers. He wants you to rest easy and know He is with you during the event. Just knowing God is near you should make you feel at ease and help you to enjoy yourself and have a good time with your family and friends.

*****

Dear God,

Thank you for being my king over all the earth. Be with me and protect me during hard times in my life. Grant me grace to follow the path to righteousness. Amen.

NOVEMBER 19

> And he called the multitude, and said unto them, Hear, and understand: Not that which goeth into the mouth defileth a man; but that which cometh out of the mouth, this defileth a man. (Matthew 15:10–11)

Be aware of what you say to others. Understand what the words mean and the harm they can cause to a person. You may say words to a person and not realize the meaning could come out all wrong.

God wants you to speak kind words to others every day. You may think not so nice things but hold your tongue and try not to speak the unkind words.

Remember the phrase: "God loves a cheerful giver." He wants you to speak cheerful words to others. It is your gift to someone.

It may take some practice, but in the long run, kind words are an absolute must to bring others to the love of Jesus.

*****

Dear God,

Thank you for putting kind words in my mouth. Help me to be a loving servant to others as you would want me to be. Amen.

NOVEMBER 20

> For whosoever will save his life shall lose it: and whosoever will lose his life for my sake shall find it. For what is a man profited, if he shall gain the whole world, and lose his own soul? Or what shall a man give in exchange for his soul? (Matthew 16:25–26)

Let God be God in your life. You could lose your soul with worldly things. Life is precious; do not give it away.

Do not take life for granted. It could be taken from you tomorrow.

God wants you to enjoy life to the fullest. Live today as if it may be your last. Share God's love with others around you.

God gave you His love to share with others. Do something nice for someone and see how good it makes you feel. God's blessings.

*****

Dear God,

Thank you for being in my life. Do not let worldly things rule my life. Be with me and strengthen me to share your love with others. Amen.

NOVEMBER 21

> His lord said unto him, Well done, good and faithful serv-ant; thou hast been faithful over a few things, I will make thee ruler over many things: enter thou into the joy of thy Lord. (Matthew 25:23)

God encourages you to be a faithful and humble servant. There should be joy in serving your Lord. He gives you Christ's joy here on earth.

How do you serve God faithfully here on earth? Do you have daily devotions or attend a Bible class at church? Or do you lead a Bible study with a group of friends each week? Whatever your calling is, to God be the glory that you are serving Him in your life.

God wants you to witness to others so all the world may know of his bountiful mercy and grace. God shines down on you with His love and wants you to pass that love on to others in this world.

*****

Dear God,

Thank you for being my faithful and humble mentor. Please show me that humbleness so that I may show love to others. Amen.

NOVEMBER 22

> And there came a voice from heaven, saying, Thou art my beloved Son, in whom I am well pleased. (Mark 1:11)

This is God's voice speaking of his beloved son in whom He is well pleased. This was said by God after the heavens were opened and the Spirit like a dove descended upon Jesus after he was baptized.

What does baptism mean to you? It is a special time when a child or adult is brought before God to be baptized with water and with the Holy Spirit. There may be sponsors in attendance at the event.

It may be the second-most important event in your life besides your birthday. Not many people know their baptismal day. It may be worth checking out when your baptismal day occurred.

This is an important day in your life, and you may want to observe it along with your birthday. It's the day you became God's child through Holy Baptism.

*****

Dear God,

Thank you for sending Jesus into my life. Help me to remember to observe my baptismal day every year, the same as I celebrate my birthday. Amen.

NOVEMBER 23

> And he took a child and set him in the midst of them: and when he had taken him in his arms, he said unto them, Whosoever shall receive one of such children in my name, receiveth me: and whosoever shall receive me, re-ceiveth not me, but him that sent me. (Mark 9:36–37)

Children are precious in God's sight. He refers to them as lambs in his fold. He wants you to have the mind like a child and be willing to learn new things as a child does. Children are open to new ideas and new adventures. Let the child inside of you come out.

It is interesting to observe the firsts for a child: first steps they take, first words they say, and even the first hugs they give to a family member. All these firsts are precious in God's eyes.

The next time you are around young children, observe how they behave and react. You may just learn something new on how to be more carefree and not worry about things. Take time to take in happiness and the nature around you that God has created; it's beautiful.

*****

Dear God,

Thank you for providing children in this world for me to learn lessons of life from. Grant me patience to be more like a child and to want to learn more about you. Amen.

NOVEMBER 24

> And one of the scribes came, and having heard them reasoning together, and perceiving that he had answered them well, asked him, Which is the first commandment of all? And Jesus answered him, the first of all the commandments is, Hear, O Israel; The Lord our God is one Lord: And shou shalt love the Lord thy God with all thy heart, and with all thy soul, and with all thy mind, and with all thy strength: this is the first commandment. And the second is like, namely this, Thou shalt love thy neigh-bour as thyself. There is none other commandment greater than these. (Mark 12:28–31)

The greatest commandment is about loving one God, showing brotherly love to everyone, and a duty to your neighbors to care for property and belongings.

Sometimes it may be a tough job showing brotherly love to those around you every day. If you start with small gestures, it can become more natural to show love on a daily basis.

The first commandment is a good one with which to start each day with.

*****

Dear God,

Thank you for giving me the first commandment. Give me strength to keep your commandments while I am on this earth. Amen.

NOVEMBER 25

> And suddenly there was with the angel a multitude of the heavenly host praising God, and saying, Glory to God in the highest, and on earth peace, good will toward men. (Luke 2:13–14)

Glorifying God with heavenly joy and heavenly praise is the song of the angels. Oh, to hear the angels shout for joy; it must have been quite a spectacle to behold.

How do you shout for joy or glorify God? Do you let your voice be heard while singing songs in church? Or are you one of the skilled choir members who can carry a tune or read notes in a songbook? Whatever your musical talent is, praise be to God you have a talent for music. Some people only get to hear the music and songs, while others can sing and use musical instruments.

Blessed be to God if you have the natural talent of music. You are a gift from above and everyone enjoys you blessing the rest of the world.

*****

Dear God,

Thank you for allowing me to praise you, O Most High. Keep me in your care and protection and never let me waiver from your flock. Amen.

NOVEMBER 26

> Then said he, Unto what is the kingdom of God like? And whereunto shall I resemble it? It is like a grain of mustard seed, which a man took, and cast into his garden; and it grew, and waxed a great tree; and the fouls of the air lodged in the branches of it. (Luke 13:18–19)

This is the parable of the mustard seed. It describes the kingdom of heaven and its magnitude and growth of the kingdom. Can you imagine the various creations God made when he created the earth?

From just a grain of a mustard seed a garden grew, and it could also relate to a field of crops growing to feed the entire community.

If you have a garden, then you know the vast amount of food that can be produced. The vegetables are a good source of nourishment for a family. A lot of times there may be an abundance in a person's garden, and they donate to a food shelter to help feed more people. God's creation is spectacular, and you should marvel at it every day.

*****

Dear God,

Thank you for sharing with me the beauty of the mustard seed and a glimpse of the beauty of the kingdom of heaven. Grant me grace to know and do your will. Amen.

NOVEMBER 27

> Saying, Go unto this people, and say, Hearing ye shall hear, and shall not understand; and seeing ye shall see, and not perceive: For the heart of this people is waxed gross, and their ears are dull of hearing and their eyes have they closed; lest they should see with their eyes, and hear with their ears, and understand with their heart, and should be converted, and I should heal them. (Acts 28:26–27)

These verses talk about the spirit's deafness, the spirit's ignorance, and the spirit's blindness, deterioration, insensibility, and neglect of salvation.

God wants His people to understand there is love in this world. You can only hope for the best of things around you. You don't want to wish harm on anyone.

Let the peace of God be your understanding to what good things are in this world and the beauty it could become if everyone showed more kindness to one another instead of causing sin to happen.

*****

Dear God,

Thank you for forgiving my sin and making me new again. Sin is a constant occurrence, but thanks be to God our sins are taken away by Jesus dying on the cross. Be with me and grant me strength to further your kingdom while I am on this earth. Amen.

NOVEMBER 28

> Then spake Jesus again unto them, saying, I am the light of the world: he that followeth me shall not walk in darkness, but shall have the light of life. (John 8:12)

Jesus talks about the rising sun. Christ is the light of the world. The verse talks about the followers of Christ and the discipleship within. Be aware of the darkness in the world. Look up to the light of life God has promised you.

Are you a light of the world? Do you shine your faith to others around you? Being a leader in your faith is a special trait one can possess. If you want to let your light shine, start today by joining a Bible class or a group study at your church.

You will be amazed at the knowledge you will obtain from others who have additional Bible expertise. Take advantage of any opportunities available to explore the Bible more.

*****

Dear God,

Thank you for being my light of the world and enlightening me on Bible study. Give me strength to continue on my journey of sharing your love with others. Amen.

NOVEMBER 29

> Saying, Blessed are they whose iniquities are forgiven, and whose sins are covered. Blessed is the man to whom the Lord will not impute sin. (Romans 4:7–8)

God's word is needed daily, not just on Sundays. This passage talks about forgiveness; if you confess your sins, God will forgive you and cleanse you from all unrighteousness.

You are truly blessed to know your sins are wiped away every day, even though sin happens constantly. Life happens, and along the way, sin also seems to happen.

God knows your every thought and action. Give Him the opportunity to enter into your life and guide you with the spirit. With God's help, you will be able to share God's love with others and let them know their sins are forgiven if they just believe in Him.

*****

Dear God,

Thank you for blessing me in my life. Thank you also for forgiving my sins when I do wrong. Be with me and guide me to follow your path to eternal life. Amen.

NOVEMBER 30

> Rejoice with them that do rejoice, and weep with them that weep. Be of the same mind one toward another. Mind not high things but condescend to men of low estate. Be not wise in your own conceits. (Romans 12:15–16)

Rejoicing and sympathizing go hand-in-hand in this verse. Everyone speaks the same language, with no divisions among people and being of the same mind and the same judgment.

Do you have that compassion for one another? God wants you to love one another, to be kind and courteous to everyone you meet.

Pride and humility shows everyone can be lifted up in God's likeness. Give God the credit! You can be proud that God gives grace to his humble people. Be proud of who you are and what you have become in Christ.

*****

Dear God,

Thank you for rejoicing and sympathizing with me in my life. You alone give me the power of humility when life gets tough. Strengthen me to go out into the world and show your love to others I meet on my journey in life. Amen.

DECEMBER 1

> Go thy way, eat thy bread with joy, and drink thy wine with a merry heart; for God now accepteth thy works. (Ecclesiastes 9:7)

Enjoy the good in this life. Life goes by too fast. The nourishment from the bread you eat each day can strengthen your heart. You need to keep your heart strong and stay mentally alert to tackle life's challenges faced every day.

God says it's okay to enjoy your wine, just know when to stop drinking. Excessive drinking can lead to bad situations. Wine is associated with being merry and having a good time; controlling the amount consumed is the key.

So go and have a good time and know that life is full of joy and happy times. God's blessings.

*****

Dear God,

Thank you for putting joy in my heart. Grant me your grace and understanding to continue serving you in Your kingdom until eternal life. Amen.

DECEMBER 2

> This wisdom have I seen also under the sun,
> and it seemed great unto me. (Ecclesiastes 9:13)

God provides wisdom, strength and understanding to His people on their journey through life.

How do you use your wisdom from God? Some may teach others about Jesus. Some may go back to school to learn new processes and procedures. Or some may use their skills on the job every day making people's lives better if they are a doctor or a nurse.

Everyone has a unique way of using their wisdom in life. If you want to learn a new skill or trade, now is a good time to start. Set your mind on trying a new adventure. You may just surprise yourself with how successful you may become.

*****

Dear God,

Thank you for giving me wisdom from above. Guide me to follow your path to righteousness until I reach my eternal home with you. Amen.

DECEMBER 3

> For thou art my hope, O Lord God: thou
> art my trust from my youth. (Psalm 71:5)

Our trust is in the Lord and whose hope the Lord is. We may be young, but having hope can get you through a lot of tribulations in life. Life is full of hopes and joys, then along the way of life, bumps occur, and it makes you stop and think.

You may need to slow down and not take life for granted. You may realize how special a family member is if a bad event happened to them. Spending time with those you love is important.

Make a list of people you may want to contact, to keep in touch with, if you haven't seen them in a while. Friendships are important; don't lose touch. Create special times with friends, such as getting together for lunch or taking in a movie or concert. These are the memories you look back upon and make you happy.

*****

Dear God,

Thank you for giving me hope and trust in you. Be with me to know and do your will as you would want me to. Amen.

DECEMBER 4

> There is nothing better for a man, than that he should eat and drink, and that he should make his soul enjoy good in his labor. This also I saw that it was from the hand of God. (Ecclesiastes 2:24)

God is giving you love. Love you should share with others. Life goes by very quickly; enjoy the ride.

God instructs you to enjoy eating and drinking with your family and friends. The socializing is good for your soul.

In the spirit of the Christmas season, people get together more often. It's a time to celebrate Jesus's birth and see family who may be a longer distance away from you.

For this holiday season, do something special with your family to honor Christmas. Since "He is the reason for the season," maybe volunteer to work at a soup kitchen or sponsor a family in need. It will make an impact on your life if you think more of others at this time of year.

*****

Dear God,

Thank you for giving me your love and compassion. Be with me and guide me on my journey to eternal life with you. Amen.

DECEMBER 5

> For God giveth to a man that is good in his sight wisdom, and knowledge, and joy: but to the sinner he giveth travail, to gather and to heap up, that he may give to him that is good before God. This also is vanity and vexation of spirit. (Ecclesiastes 2:26)

God speaks about being obedient and then promises wisdom and joy thereafter.

Sin brings consequences. Romans 6:23 says, "For the wages of sin is death; but the gift of God is eternal life through Jesus Christ our Lord." This refers to sin's penalty; but Christ is life.

This passage also ties into the worldly care aspect. Various cares of the world include walking in vain, sleepless nights, and deceitfulness of riches.

Pray to God for wisdom and knowledge and joy that your life may be filled with happiness all year through. God's blessings.

*****

Dear God,

Thank you for the wisdom, joy, and knowledge you have showered upon me. Grant me your grace to know and do your will and follow your path of righteousness. Amen.

DECEMBER 6

> The Lord is my light and my salvation;
> whom shall I fear? The Lord is the strength of
> my life; of whom shall I be afraid? (Psalm 27:1)

God shines a light of salvation upon you. He is your strength, and you can trust in Him to give you the courage to get you through life's challenges every day.

What gives you strength? Could it be the Spirit breathing new life in you? Or could it be your open heart accepting Jesus as your Lord and Savior.

Whatever your strength is, show your compassion to others by doing good deeds for them. Maybe offering to give someone a ride to church or offering to do an errand for a shut-in. All these kind gestures are a way to show your love and God's salvation to others.

Let your light shine and be the brightness in someone's life today.

*****

Dear God,

Thank you for being my light and my salvation. Be with me and guide me on my journey to eternal life. Amen.

DECEMBER 7

> *It is God that girdeth me with strength, and*
> *maketh my way perfect. (Psalm 18:32)*

God promises to give you strength and asks you to follow a life of kindness, compassion, and grace.

It seems like a tall order to follow. But with God's help, he will guide you down the right path.

Reading scripture and obeying his commandments is a good start.

God understands you are not perfect, and He knows everyone sins. But thanks be to God, Jesus died to take away your sin and make you new again.

So the next time you sin, thank God for sending his Son to wash away your sin.

*****

Dear God,

Thank you for giving me strength and showing me I am not perfect in your eyes. Give me peace and understanding to show love to others the way you would want me to do. Amen.

DECEMBER 8

> Forbearing one another, and forgiving one another, if any man have a quarrel against any: even as Christ forgave you, so also do ye.
> (Colossians 3:13)

Forgiveness means forbearing one another and showing mercy to others as God shows compassion on you. God is the gift of love. God forgave iniquity and turned his anger away from the unjust.

Take a lesson from God and show tenderheartedness when you see someone suffering. Be a good friend. If you had a struggle, you would want someone to show compassion to you also.

As the saying goes, "Forgive and forget." God wants you to forgive someone when they do you harm. It's the Christian thing to do.

Showing kindness never hurt anyone. Try showing kindness to someone today; maybe just a simple smile may make someone's day. God's blessings.

*****

Dear God,

Thank you for showing kindness to me and forgiving me my sins. Guide me through life's struggles to my eternal home. Amen.

DECEMBER 9

> Teach me thy way, O Lord; I will walk in thy truth: unite my heart to fear thy name.
> (Psalm 86:11)

God wants to teach you various lessons from the Bible. He may refer to you as becoming little children as in the Bible or exhibiting the action like one of the disciples.

He wants you to take heed while He teaches you and for you to walk in his truth. He offers the kingdom of heaven to those who believe.

Are you walking in God's truth? Do you show love and compassion to those around you? If not, why not start your walk with God today. There is no better time than the present. God is your guide, and you can follow his example.

*****

Dear God,

Thank you for teaching me the way in your truth. Guide me to follow your example and show love to one another. Amen.

DECEMBER 10

> Let everything that hath breath praise the
> Lord. Praise ye the Lord. (Psalm 150:6)

Praising the Lord can be achieved in a variety of formats. It can even be done with a psaltery or a harp.

As mentioned in 1 Peter 2:9, "But ye are a chosen generation, a royal priesthood, a holy nation...who hath called you out of darkness into his marvelous light." It is an honor to praise the Lord.

How do you praise the Lord? Is it with your voice or do you have a musical instrument? If you have a musical instrument, you are very talented. Or if you sing in the church choir, you also have a gift of using your voice.

Everyone has different talents and gifts. God made everyone unique. If you have a gift from God, use it to bring others to the Word. Your talent may not seem special to you, but in God's eyes it is. Let your light shine so others will be drawn to Jesus.

*****

Dear God,

Thank you for giving me breath to praise the Lord. Grant me grace to continue serving you while I live on this earth. Amen.

DECEMBER 11

> For if ye forgive men their trespasses, your heavenly Father will also forgive you: But if ye forgive not men their trespasses, neither will your Father forgive your trespasses. (Matthew 6:14–15)

These verses speak about forgiveness and promise mercy. As Psalm 103:8 says, "The Lord is merciful and gracious, slow to anger, and plenteous in mercy." He shows you his mercy and grace.

Forgiveness may sometimes be tough to do. When someone does something bad to you, you may not want to forgive that person right away. You may need to pray about it and ask God for compassion. And forgiving someone may take time; it may not happen overnight.

*****

Dear God,

Thank you for forgiving my sins when I have been in difficult situations. Guide me to follow your path to eternal life. Amen.

DECEMBER 12

> So then faith cometh by hearing, and hearing by the word of God. (Romans 10:17)

This passage talks about faith and God's word. Faith is very powerful. You live by faith—it purifies your heart, it is counted for righteousness, and it worketh by love.

Everyone has some form of faith. Some people have a stronger faith than others. When you are faced with a challenging medical diagnosis, it is your faith that pulls you through. Some say God only gives you what you can handle. You may think there is no end to your suffering, but God is with you all the way.

It's faith that sustains you to keep going when the road gets tough. It's faith that will keep your head up in your dark days.

Keep the faith and continue praying to God for comfort. He hears your prayer and will provide an answer in due time.

*****

Dear God,

Thank you for giving me faith to hear Your Word. Grant me peace and understanding to follow your path to righteousness. Amen.

DECEMBER 13

> For the Lord giveth wisdom: out of his mouth cometh knowledge and understanding. He layeth up sound wisdom for the righteous: he is a buckler to them that walk up-rightly.
> (Proverbs 2:6–7)

This passage speaks of wisdom promised, God's Word as a light, the righteous, God as a shield, and God as the divine keeper.

God is all-powerful and does provide for His people. Take heed of all the ways God shows his power.

You would be lucky to have just one of those traits. That's why God is who He is. You can never be Him, but you can serve Him and be in His kingdom.

If you could have God's wisdom, what would you change in the world? Some may say hatred or wickedness. Some may say war between countries. Or some may say peace and love to all mankind.

*****

Dear God,

Thank you for giving me wisdom and knowledge. Grant me grace to follow your path to my eternal home. Amen.

DECEMBER 14

> The meek shall eat and be satisfied: they
> shall praise the Lord that seek him: your heart
> shall live forever. (Psalm 22:26)

The people who seek meekness shall inherit the earth and delight in the abundance of peace. There is a promise to seekers. If the people humble themselves and turn away from their wicked ways, God will forgive their sin and heal them.

Is it your intention to seek God and His Word? Being humble is not as easy as one may think. Everyone is tempted by material things in this world. Knowing when to turn away from the evil is what's important.

God's saving grace is there for the taking. Ask God for His compassion and understanding to help you on your journey. The journey could be long or short, depending on your situation. Everyone has different circumstances in life. May God give you the direction you are counting on.

*****

Dear God,

Thank you for showing me meekness in life. You alone have the power to grant wisdom and understanding. Be with me to follow your path to eternal life. Amen.

DECEMBER 15

> But as it is written, eye hath not seen, nor ear heard, neither have entered into the heart of man, the things which God hath prepared for them that love him. (1 Corinthians 2:9)

Love for God is the crucial point emphasized in this verse. The verse also speaks about the lack of Spirit insight, secret things, and Divine Preparation.

Have you prepared yourself for Christ? Yes, there is preparation. Yes, there is the spirit which holds all the secret truths. But you can have the Spirit within you by just believing in Jesus.

Jesus is the one true God, who died on the cross for you. Give Him the glory and your life will change for the better.

Commit your life to Christ and be a living example of God's saving grace to you.

*****

Dear God,

Thank you for loving me even though I am a sinful human being. Grant me grace and mercy to follow your path to righteousness. Amen.

DECEMBER 16

> For I am not ashamed of the gospel of Christ: for it is the power of God unto salvation to everyone that believeth; to the Jew first, and also to the Greek. (Romans 1:16)

This verse speaks about the "Power of the Word," which includes:

1. a devouring flame—words in thy mouth turn into fire.
2. a crushing hammer—hammer that crushes a rock into pieces.
3. a life-giving force—as prophesied, a noise, shaking and then bones coming together.
4. a saving power—salvation for all believers.
5. a defensive weapon—the sword of the spirit.
6. a probing instrument—the word of God is quick and powerful and sharper than a sword piercing the soul.

This verse also relates to the saving faith all believers have through eternal life. As a believer, you can be assured the benefits of heaven someday as a child of God. God's blessings.

*****

Dear God,

Thank you for giving me the "Power of the Word" in my life. Grant me your grace to follow your example pure. Amen.

DECEMBER 17

> Verily, verily, I say unto you, He that heareth my word, and believeth on him that sent me, hath everlasting life, and shall not come into condemnation; but is passed from death unto life. (John 5:24)

This passage speaks of eternal life. It also refers to a promise to believers and the saving faith.

Do you have the saving faith to which Jesus refers to? Jesus says, if you hear the Word and believe it, then everlasting life shall come to you.

This reward of salvation is a gift from God for his people. Jesus died on the cross to save your sins, and you have the assurance that your sins are forgiven. Open your heart and let Jesus in. You are renewed by his salvation. Glorify God for giving you that saving faith.

*****

Dear God,

Keep me in your faith and guide me in your direction to be your faithful servant. Amen.

DECEMBER 18

> If ye keep my commandments, ye shall abide in my love; even as I have kept my Father's commandments and abide in his love. (John 15:10)

Christ's command is to love one another and believe on the name of Jesus Christ. He gave the commandments as a guideline by which to live your life. Believing these commandments and then living your life by them may be two different things. People may believe the commandments to be true. Now God wants you to focus on the true meaning of each commandment.

As the verse talks about abiding in love…do you abide in Christ's love in your life? Do you show that true love to your family members? You may say you love them, but do you show it in your everyday living? God has blessed you with a loving family; people who care very deeply for your well-being.

Starting today, show your family more love and affection than you might have shown them yesterday. Try turning over a new leaf and show more love to other members of your family as well. You will be surprised at the difference it makes for you and maybe they will pass on the same love to others.

*****

Dear God,

Thank you for giving me your commandments to live my life by. Keep me strong in your ways and teach me to show your abiding love to others. Amen.

DECEMBER 19

> For God, who commanded the light to shine out of dark-ness, hath shined in our hearts, to give the light of the knowledge of the glory of God in the face of Jesus Christ. (2 Corinthians 4:6)

Christ is the light of the world. He shines his light and knowledge down to you to provide enlightenment so you can believe in Him. His glory and honor are yours through eternal salvation. God's salvation is real. You are saved from the devil and all his wicked ways.

Do you shine your light among your family and friends? Do you set an example of Christlike behavior to others? Others see you every day; be the face so they want to be like Christ in their life.

If your light is not shining, starting today, do nice things for those close to you. A simple smile or hug is all you need to give. Show others you care about their well-being. Be interested in their life.

*****

Dear God,

Thank you for shining your light upon me. Be with me to shine my light to others to spread your love. Amen.

DECEMBER 20

> And he said unto his disciples, Therefore I say unto you, Take no thought for your life, what ye shall eat; neither for the body, what ye shall put on. The life is more than meat, and the body is more than raiment. (Luke 12:22–23)

This passage talks about your appetite being restrained. You worry about what you should eat. God doesn't want you to worry; he provides your daily food.

You also should not worry about your clothes; they are not a concern when you get to heaven.

God wants you to focus on living your life to be pleasing to Him. Don't worry about material things; concentrate more on showing God's grace and love to others.

Take an interest in those around you. They are the people that ask you every day, "How are you doing today?" Turn around and reciprocate the gesture to them. It's surprising what you can learn about others when you start to ask about their well-being.

*****

Dear God,

Thank you for giving me an appetite for life. Show me your love and grace to always care about others. Amen.

DECEMBER 21

> Cast thy burden upon the Lord, and he shall sustain thee: he shall never suffer the righteous to be moved. (Psalm 55:22)

Christ carried the burdens of humanity. He bore your grief and carried your sorrows. He took your infirmities and bore your sicknesses. And ultimately, he died on the cross to save you and forgive all your sins.

Christ is also your Divine Support. He is your refuge and your everlasting arm among the evil foes. He is your shield of salvation and holds you up when you are down. His grace is over you protecting you from harm's way.

Look up to God when times get tough and ask for his strength and compassion. God's blessings.

*****

Dear God,

Thank you for carrying my burdens for me. Grant me refuge and provide your shield of salvation on my journey through life. Amen.

DECEMBER 22

> Train up a child in the way he should go:
> and when he is old, he will not depart from it.
> (Proverbs 22:6)

As a parent, it is your duty to train, to nurture, to provide for, to control, and to love your children. These are the duties incumbent upon parents.

God wants you to teach your children diligently and also to nurture them in the admonition of the Lord.

When you were young, your parents probably gave you a lot of advice, in addition to some scolding at times. As you got older, you may have realized your parents did have some good advice for you. Then it came time to raise your own children. How did you raise your children? Were you strict or more lenient with your children? And then came being a grandparent. Some say being a grandparent is the easiest task. Giving advice is natural as you become more relaxed.

*****

Dear God,

Thank you for training me to be a child of God. Be with me as I train my children and grandchildren in the admonition of the Lord. Amen.

DECEMBER 23

> Know therefore that the Lord thy God, he is God, the faithful God, which keepeth covenant and mercy with them that love him and keep his commandments to a thousand generations. (Deuteronomy 7:9)

Divine faithfulness reaches all God's people for thousands of generations. His mercy will He keep forever more and the covenant will stand tall with Him also. God does ask His people to promise to be obedient to him.

Have you kept God's covenant? Have you been faithful to God throughout your life? Being faithful is a difficult task for Christians. Everyone gets tempted by not only lusts and other sins of the world, including being tempted by the devil. You may be tempted to go the opposite direction that God wants you to go. It takes a strong faith to stay on the path that is right.

Being faithful means dedicating your life to God and letting him take over your life. It can be a big change in your life. Open your heart and wait to see what good things God can do for you.

*****

Dear God,

Thank you for giving me your commandments to follow. Keep me in your faith so I may continue following you on my journey through life. Amen.

DECEMBER 24

> For this is good and acceptable in the sight of God our Savior; Who will have all men to be saved, and to come unto the knowledge of the truth. (1 Timothy 2:3–4)

We seek the salvation of God. Having the Spiritual knowledge of God leads you to be obedient and in turn leads to eternal life.

As mentioned in John 8:31–32, "Then said Jesus to those Jews which believed on him, if ye continue in my Word, then are ye my disciplines indeed; and ye shall know the truth, and the truth shall make you free." This is truly liberating your soul from all error.

God wants you to have wisdom and understanding and come to the knowledge of the truth. Do you feel you have the salvation of God? Believing in God's Word is a start.

The Bible is your source to gain more knowledge. It's there for your reading. It's never too late to start reading your Bible every day. The knowledge that you will gain will be immeasurable. God's blessings.

*****

Dear God,

Thank you for giving me salvation. Please provide me the Spiritual knowledge to as I read the Bible daily. Amen.

DECEMBER 25

> For unto you is born this day in the city of David a Savior, which is Christ the Lord. (Luke 2:11)

This verse talks about Jesus, the Messiah. Also, relating to this verse is Matthew 11:3, "Art thou he that should come, or do we look for another?"

Jesus is truly the long-awaited Savior of the world. He came into the world to seek the lost and the erring. He came into the world to give hope, joy, and peace to all people.

What would you say to Jesus if you met Him today? It's something to think about. Everyone can say a prayer to God but to actually have a conversation would be truly remarkable.

God's blessings.

*****

Dear God,

Thank you for sending Jesus to be my Savior. Grant me peace and understanding to know and do your will until be meet in heaven someday. Amen.

DECEMBER 26

> Now there hearken unto me, O ye children: for blessed are they that keep my ways. Hear instruction, and be wise, and refuse it not. (Proverbs 8:32–33)

This passage speaks about the promise to children. It refers to the children as the "blessed ones." It encourages obedience among the children and gives instructions for life to God's people.

Some of the instructions and promises from God to his children include:

- Being reverent children—honoring thy father and thy mother
- Lambs of the flock—feeds the flock like a shepherd, gathers them up with his arms, and gently leads them
- Little children—let the children come to God and his kingdom
- Children of believers—all are promised the kingdom of God who believe

God wants young and old to believe in His Word. It's never too late to start believing in God.

*****

Dear God,

Thank you for bringing salvation to me when I was young. Be with me and keep me faithful on my journey to eternal life. Amen.

DECEMBER 27

> Beloved, let us love one another: for love is of God; and everyone that loveth is born of God, and knoweth God. He that loveth not knoweth not God; for God is love. (1 John 4:7–8)

Brotherly love comes in various forms: fervent, abounding, sincere, Christ's love, unselfish, impartial, and love of discipleship. Basically, God wants you to love one another and also to love thy neighbor as thyself. To love one another fervently with a pure heart.

What kind of love do you share with others? Maybe you display all these forms, or maybe one or two. God encourages you to show love to all people.

Showing loving kindness, judgment, and righteousness to others demonstrates God's grace. Obedience comes with the condition of receiving Christ into your life. Live a life that is well-pleasing to God.

*****

Dear God,

Thank you for showing me brotherly love. Grant me grace and mercy as I show love to others on this earth. Amen.

DECEMBER 28

> The Lord is good unto them that wait for him, to the soul that seeketh him. (Lamentations 3:25)

Repentance may be the first thought when one is in trouble. God asks that you keep his commandments while living on this earth.

You should also wait for God. Waiting patiently for His mercy to be upon you. God does wait patiently for you and hears your cry when you need help or are in trouble.

What good things have you received from God in the past? Maybe it was good news you received when you had a medical test and were anxious about the results. Or maybe it was a job interview you had and you waited patiently to hear if you received the new position. Whatever the cause, God wants you to wait patiently for the result.

Patience is a virtue. It may not come easy for everyone. If you are a parent, you need a lot of patience raising children. Give God the glory and ask for His guiding hand to get you through the tough days at hand.

*****

Dear God,

Thank you for your goodness you have shown to me in my life. Protect me and guide me to follow your ways as I make my journey through life. Amen.

DECEMBER 29

> Blessed is the man that endureth temptation;: for when he is tried, he shall receive the crown of life, which the Lord hath promised to them that love him. (James 1:12)

You need God's Word every day. You should trust in God to give you his grace and mercy. You can choose God to provide for your every need. God satisfies you with a home to live in and food to eat. What a blessing that God provides for you.

You may experience temptations in your life; look to God for guidance, so you can follow the path to righteousness. He alone knows your thoughts and actions; call upon Him when in trouble.

As the verse says, "Receive the crown of life, which the Lord has promised to them that love Him."

The Crown of Life is yours since Jesus died on the cross to take away your sins. What wonderful news it is to know every day you can wake up knowing it's a new day in your life. Make each day special, knowing it's a fresh start with new opportunities to share God's love with others.

*****

Dear God,

Thank you for blessing me every day and for giving me a Crown of Life. You alone have the power to give me your grace and mercy. Help me share your love with others on this earth. Amen.

DECEMBER 30

> But I say unto you, Love your enemies, bless them that curse you, do good to them that hate you, and pray for them which despitefully use you, and persecute you. (Matthew 5:44–45)

The Authority of Christ is evident in this verse. He has the power over heaven and earth. He executes judgment because He is the Son of Man.

You should show good for evil. If your enemy is hungry, give him food. If He is thirsty, give Him drink. God wants you to love your enemies, bless them that curse you, and do good to them that hate you.

You were put on this earth to be kind to others. Practice that kindness every day, and you will be amazed how fulfilled your life will become.

*****

Dear God,

Thank you for giving me the authority of Christ in my life. Bless me to be a servant of your love to others and share kindness to everyone I meet. Amen.

DECEMBER 31

> But I trust I shall shortly see thee, and we shall speak face to face. Peace be to thee. Our friends salute thee. Greet the friends by name. (3 John 1:14)

This is the last devotion for the year. The verse says, "I shall shortly see thee," and could be applied to seeing Jesus in heaven.

Are you prepared to see Jesus on your last day on earth? There may be many things you want to do yet while you live on this earth. Some people have a bucket list of things they want to accomplish. If you have any unfinished business, you may want to get them started, as tomorrow is a new year, with new opportunity.

You do not know when your last day on earth is, but when your time does come and you meet Jesus, greet Him with open arms, as He will lead you to your new heavenly home.

You will be at peace with Jesus in heaven. There will be no pain or suffering, only joy and happiness. You will be greeted by your family and friends who went to heaven before you. You can look forward to your eternal home, to be with Jesus. God bless you on your journey through life.

*****

Dear God,

Thank you for giving me life on this earth. Be with me as I continue my journey through life until I reach my heavenly home. Amen.

BONNIE'S KEYS TO LIFE

- Place God first.
- Always love one another.
- Resist hate.
- Practice generosity.
- Simple living is best.
- Pray to forgive quickly.
- Let kindness rule.

Father's Love Letter - An intimate message from God to you.

My Child,

You may not know me, but I know everything about you. Psalm 139:1 I know when you sit down and when you rise up. Psalm 139:2 I am familiar with all your ways. Psalm 139:3 Even the very hairs on your head are numbered. Matthew 10:29-31 For you were made in my image. Genesis 1:27 In me you live and move and have your being. Acts 17:28 For you are my offspring. Acts 17:28 I knew you even before you were conceived. Jeremiah 1:4-5 I chose you when I planned creation. Ephesians 1:11-12 You were not a mistake, for all your days are written in my book. Psalm 139:15-16 I determined the exact time of your birth and where you would live. Acts 17:26 You are fearfully and wonderfully made. Psalm 139:14 I knit you together in your mother's womb. Psalm 139:13 And brought you forth on the day you were born. Psalm 71:6 I have been misrepresented by those who don't know me. John 8:41-44 I am not distant and angry, but am the complete expression of love. 1 John 4:16 And it is my desire to lavish my love on you. Simply because you are my child and I am your Father. 1 John 3:1 I offer you more than your earthly father ever could. Matthew 7:11 For I am the perfect Father. Matthew 5:48 Every good gift you receive comes from my hand. James 1:17 For I am your provider and I meet all your needs. Matthew 6:31-33 My plan for your future has always been filled with hope. Jeremiah 29:11 Because I love you with an everlasting love. Jeremiah 31:3 My thoughts toward you are countless as the sand on the seashore. Psalm 139:17-18 And I rejoice over you with singing. Zephaniah 3:17 I will never stop doing good to you. Jeremiah 32:40 For you are my treasured possession. Exodus 19:5 I desire to establish you with all my heart and all my soul. Jeremiah 32:41 And I want to show you great and marvelous things. Jeremiah 33:3 If you seek me with all your heart, you will find me. Deuteronomy 4:29 Delight in me and I will give you the desires of your heart. Psalm 37:4 For it is I who gave you those desires. Philippians 2:13 I am able to do more for you than you could possibly imagine. Ephesians 3:20 For I am your greatest encourager. 2 Thessalonians 2:16-17 I am also the Father who comforts you in all your troubles. 2 Corinthians 1:3-4 When you are brokenhearted, I am close to you. Psalm 34:18 As a shepherd carries a lamb, I have carried you close to my heart. Isaiah 40:11 One day, I will wipe away every tear from your eyes. And I'll take away all the pain you have suffered on this earth. Revelation 21:3-4 I am your Father, and I love you even as I love my son, Jesus. John 17:23 For in Jesus, my love for you is revealed. John 17:26 He is the exact representation of my being. Hebrews 1:3 He came to demonstrate that I am for you, not against you. Romans 8:31 And to tell you that I am not counting your sins. 2 Corinthians 5:18-19 Jesus died so that you and I could be reconciled. 2 Corinthians 5:18-19 His death was the ultimate expression of my love for you. 1 John 4:10 I gave up everything I loved that I might gain your love. Romans 8:31-32 If you receive the gift of my son Jesus, you receive me. 1 John 2:23 And nothing will ever separate you from my love again. Romans 8:38-39 Come home and I'll throw the biggest party heaven has ever seen. Luke 15:7 I have always been Father, and will always be Father. Ephesians 3:14-15 My question is... Will you be my child? John 1:12-13 I am waiting for you. Luke 15:11-32

Love, Your Dad... Almighty God

Father's Love Letter used by permission Father Heart Communications
©1999 FathersLoveLetter.com (Please feel free to copy & share with others)

ABOUT THE AUTHOR

Bonnie Weber enjoys studying the Bible and sharing her faith with others. She attends various Bible classes at her church. She is active in her church, serving on the women's board and also serving funeral luncheons.

Sharing God's Word with others is a special mission of hers. The mission field is plentiful, and she hopes to bring the lost and erring to know God.

Bonnie resides in Michigan with her husband of forty-five years, Scott. Her pride and joy are her four grandchildren.

www.ingramcontent.com/pod-product-compliance
Lightning Source LLC
Chambersburg PA
CBHW031058210225
22236CB00002B/2